THE MOUNTIES
MASSACRE IN THE HILLS

Also available in the Target series:

THE MOUNTIES—THE GREAT MARCH WEST
Terrance Dicks

in preparation:

THE MOUNTIES—WARDRUMS OF THE
BLACKFOOT
Terrance Dicks

THE MOUNTIES

MASSACRE
IN THE HILLS

TERRANCE DICKS

First published simultaneously in Great Britain by
Tandem Publishing Ltd, and Allan Wingate
(Publishers) Ltd, 1976

ISBN 0 426 11105 2

Target Books are published by Tandem Publishing Ltd.
A Howard & Wyndham Company
14 Gloucester Road, London SW7 4RD

Printed and bound in Great Britain by Richard Clay
(The Chaucer Press) Ltd, Bungay, Suffolk

Contents

The Cypress Hills Massacre

Abe Farwell stood at the gate of his trading fort and watched the line of horsemen coming towards him. He counted seven riding single file along the winding trail of Battle Creek. Seven tough, grimy, unshaven men in worn buckskins, every one armed with revolver, knife and repeating rifle. Wolf-trappers or buffalo-hunters, thought Abe. These'd want provisions, ammunition, plenty of liquor. Good customers, but ugly too, mean hard-bitten men, quick to turn violent with a drop of whisky inside them. Abe fixed a welcoming smile on his face, and hoped there wouldn't be any trouble.

'Afternoon, gentlemen. Welcome to Farwell's Fort. How's the wolfing?'

The leader of the group was a tall, thin man, with greasy yellow hair down to his shoulders and a boney skull-like face. He swung down from his horse with a grunt of weariness. 'We ain't after wolves,' he growled. He shoved past the tubby little trader, and led his horse into the compound.

The next few hours were frantically busy for Abe and his Indian wife. There were horses to be stabled and cared for, hungry men to be fed. Abe's wife, a silent, smiling Blackfoot squaw, cooked up an enormous batch of bacon and beans, with biscuits and hot coffee. When the meal was over, Abe brought out the whisky, and the men drunk thirstily from the enamel mugs. Soon the air of the Fort's big main room was thick with whisky fumes and blue with tobacco smoke.

As he cleared away the tin plates for his wife to wash, Abe studied the small group. There was Longhair, two tough-looking characters so alike they must be brothers, a fat man, a thin one with sandy hair, a nervous weak-looking man and a stocky man called Ed. As he'd guessed, they were wolfers and trappers based at Fort Benton over the border in Montana. He wondered what had brought this grim little party so far into the Cypress Hills.

It was the long-haired man, who seemed to be both leader and spokesman for the rest, who finally explained. They'd been returning to Fort Benton from a successful winter's hunting in Canada. Last camp had been made on the Teton River, no more than five miles from Fort Benton, and they'd taken a few drinks to celebrate the end of a good season.

Bitterly, the long-haired man went on. 'Seeing as we were almost home, we got careless. Didn't set a guard. Woke up next morning to find the Indians had run off our horses.'

The fat hunter took a swig of whisky and spat. 'All the horses, all the furs, all the buffalo hides. Took us all winter to get 'em. Gone in one night.'

Abe nodded sympathetically. With a good haul of hides and furs, and Fort Benton in sight, they must have felt the money was almost in their pockets.

'Mighty tough luck, gents,' he said solemnly. Although Abe didn't dare say it, he thought anyone who left horses unguarded in Indian country deserved all he got. This had been the view of the Army in Fort Benton when the angry trappers had gone to them with their story.

'Told us it was a useful lesson,' growled the sandy-haired man. 'Next time we'd know to be more careful!'

Frustrated and angry, the trappers had decided to try and recover the horses themselves. They'd managed to borrow enough money to buy ammunition, supplies and fresh horses and set out after the thieves. But even this had gone wrong for them. 'We trailed 'em into these hills,' said Long-hair disgustedly, 'then we lost the track. We was gettin' low on supplies, so we came on here. Any Indians in these parts?'

The sudden question took Abe by surprise. 'Well, there's Chief Little Soldier's people. Village of about forty lodges just the other side of the creek...'

Abe regretted the words as soon as they were spoken. The trappers lifted their heads like hungry wolves. Hastily Abe blundered on, '*They* ain't the Injuns you're looking for. These are Assiniboine— been peaceful and friendly for years. It was probably a war-party of Sioux or Cree took your horses. Young bucks out to make a name for themselves.'

'The trail was leading this way,' said Long-hair. 'Maybe they just shook us off and headed for home.'

'Listen,' said Abe, 'that *proves* they ain't the ones. No Injun leaves a trail to his own village. They'd have led you miles away, then doubled back home.

9

The ones who stole your horses are probably back in Montana by now...'

Long-hair glared at him suspiciously. 'You're mighty quick to defend these Indians. What are you—some kind of Indian-lover?'

Abe swallowed hard. In the West of the eighteen-seventies it was dangerous to stand up for the Indians—you ran the risk of being considered a traitor to your own kind. But Abe felt he had to speak out. 'I been trading with the Assiniboine for years. They always treated me square. They're good Indians.'

The fat hunter laughed gratingly. 'Ain't you heard, trader? There's only one kind of *good* Indian?' He was referring to the famous saying of General Sheridan, back in the Indian wars of the eighteen-sixties. '*The only good Indian is a dead Indian.*'

There came a sudden pounding of unshod hooves and the door was flung open. A tall figure in sheepskin war-shirt and buckskin leggings barred the doorway. He wore an ornate head-dress, and carried a long lance. This was Little Soldier, Chief of the Assiniboine. Behind in the compound a band of young warriors in breech-clout and moccasins were dismounting from wiry Indian ponies, chattering excitedly.

Suddenly the room went very quiet. Although the trappers were armed, each man kept his hand well away from gun or knife. There were at least twenty warriors outside in the compound, and the door was already open.

Ignoring the party of trappers, Little Soldier announced, 'We have good hunt. Come to trade.'

He stepped aside from the doorway, and several young braves staggered in, loaded down with piles of buffalo hides and furs. They stacked them on the floor. Abe nodded. 'The Chief is always welcome,' he said gravely.

When the hides were all delivered, Abe totalled them up and led the Chief to the store-room near by. The warriors began to carry away the chosen trade goods: sacks of flour and sugar, salt, an axe, beads and mirrors for the women, powder and bullets for the old-fashioned muzzle-loading guns of the warriors. Abe looked on, his agile mind totting up the value of the goods. When he reckoned the exchange was fair, he held up his hand. The Chief nodded to the warriors, and they left the store-room, knowing that Abe always gave fair value.

Only when the trade goods were loaded on to the ponies did Little Soldier deign to notice the hunters. He stared imperiously at them. 'You are Americans. Why do you come to my land?'

Long-hair spread out his hands and smiled easily. 'Just hunting and trapping, Chief, same as always.'

'The winter season is over. You should return to your own country, across the border.'

'That's just what we plan to do, Chief. We'll be setting off in the morning.'

Little Soldier grunted, and turned to go. Long-hair called after him. 'Say, Chief, how about a drink? Just to prove we're all good friends.' He grabbed a bottle from Abe's counter and held it out. The Chief hesitated, took the bottle, drained half at one swig and passed it back. Long-hair smiled, 'Finish the bottle, Chief, that's the style. Some for your warriors too. Here, Abe, break a case, I'll pay.' He fished out a handful of silver dollars and flung them on the bar. 'Come on, boys, pass out the booze.'

The hunters started handing bottles to the warriors, who snatched at them like greedy children. More and more warriors crowded in, and soon every one had a bottle of whisky, and was drinking eagerly.

Abe looked on in astonishment, wondering at this sudden generosity. Maybe Long-hair was frightened at seeing himself so outnumbered and was trying to buy his safety. He was wasting his money, thought Abe, since Little Soldier had no intention of harming him. Still, it was all good business.

The carousing went on for most of the night, and it was nearly dawn when the Indians mounted their ponies and rode unsteadily away. Long-hair saw them off, waving and shouting vows of friendship. When the sound of hoof-beats had died away, he came back into the trading post, slamming the door behind him. His skull-like face was set in an angry snarl. 'We'll give 'em a while to settle down,' he announced, 'then move in just before dawn.'

Abe stared in astonishment. 'Move in where?'

'You think I fed them savages good whisky for the fun of it? They'll be sleeping like hogs soon.'

Abe was still baffled. 'What are you planning to do?'

'We're gonna teach them lousy redskins to keep their hands off white men's property. They stole our horses all right. And where do you think those furs and hides came from. That's *our* stuff they traded you—ain't it boys?'

Growls of assent came from the rest of the party. They were all pretty drunk themselves by now, and their mood had suddenly turned ugly and vicious.

Abe looked at them appalled. 'That just ain't so, boys. You were robbed weeks ago, right? Those hides and furs are fresh-skinned. They *couldn't* be yours.'

Long-hair gave the little trader a shove that sent him staggering against the counter. 'You keep out of this, Indian-lover, or we'll take care of you too!'

Clutching his bruised ribs, Abe looked on helplessly as the trappers fetched ammunition from his shelves, each man loading himself down with all the shells he could carry. When everyone was ready, Long-hair spoke. 'We move out on foot. Take your time, move slow and quiet.' Abe watched as one by one the hunters slipped out into the night.

Left alone in his trading post, Abe looked round the littered room. He couldn't take in the full horror of what was happening. He considered trying to warn the Indians, but courage failed him. In their present savage mood he knew the trappers would kill him without hesitation. And there was his wife to think of, asleep in their room. She was an Indian too. Terrified, but unable to stay away, Abe slipped out after the trappers.

The party of white men moved steadily closer to the Indian village. The sound of whooping and chanting drifted towards them, as some of the Indians kept up their celebration. They took up their positions in a shallow gulley amongst the willows that lined Battle Creek. As the pale dawn light spread slowly through the sky, they could make out the Indian village, just across the creek. Long-hair waited until it was fully light then raised his hand. 'Okay, boys. Let 'em have it.'

A moment's silence, then the sudden crash of rifle fire as all seven men blazed away at the sleeping Indian village. Bullets ripped through the buffalo-hide tepees. Hidden behind a nearby tree, Abe Far-well looked on in horror.

The village was thrown into complete pandemonium. Little Soldier rolled from his blankets, grabbed his weapons and tried to rally his warriors. Most were still in a drunken sleep, and it took time to get them awake and armed. And the deadly hail of bullets continued, ripping through the village, cutting down warriors, women and children alike. Many of the Indians were killed as they slept, before Little Soldier managed to gather enough men for a counter-attack. But the white men were well positioned, crouched down in their gulley amongst the willow trees. More important, each one had a repeating rifle and plenty of ammunition. The Indians had only bows and arrows, and a few old-fashioned muzzle-loaders.

Three times Little Soldier led his warriors in a charge, splashing across the shallow creek into the fire of the hidden guns. Three times the Indians were shot down, and at the end of the third charge the body of Little Soldier lay on the heap of dead warriors.

The death of their chief broke the Indians' resistance. All those who could still walk or crawl fled their village for the hills. The guns were silent at last, and the camp lay empty, littered with the bodies of the dead.

Panting hard, Long-hair looked round his group. 'Anybody hurt?'

A voice came from the end of the line. 'Ed got it. Arrow in the throat. Reckon he's the only one though.'

Long-hair looked over the desolate village and grunted. 'Well—we showed 'em. They'll think twice before robbing another white man.'

No one replied. It was as if even these hardened men were appalled at what they had done.

They carried Ed's body back to the trading post. Finding Abe cowering in hiding on the way, they dragged him back with them. The trappers loaded their horses with furs and hides, and anything else they could carry, and then set fire to the wooden building. Abe stood watching in hopeless silence, his wife beside him, fully expecting that they would both be killed.

Long-hair jammed the muzzle of his rifle under Abe's chin. 'Just you remember what happened. We came here peaceful to trade. The Indians attacked us, burned down your post. We helped you stand them off. Remember to tell it right—or you'll get the same as your Indian friends.'

Too terrified to speak, Abe nodded dumbly and the hunters rode away, leaving him alone with Ed's body, in the blazing ruins of his trading post.

In the weeks that followed, news of the events at

Battle Creek gradually spread. In America it was hailed as the victory of dauntless frontiersmen against murdering savages. Abe Farwell had disappeared and there was no one to challenge this account. But in Canada, the Blackfoot Indians told appalled Hudson Bay traders another story. From the traders, the Government in Ottowa heard an account of the cold-blooded massacre of peaceful Indians by a band of white ruffians.

For a long time the Canadian Government had been concerned about lawlessness in its newly acquired North-West Territories. This latest incident spurred them to act. A special body of mounted riflemen was created to bring law and order to the North-West. They wore scarlet coats, because the Indians knew and respected the red coats worn by the soldiers of Her Majesty Queen Victoria. But the members of this new force were not soldiers. They were known as the North-West Mounted Police, or as they soon came to be called—the Mounties.

1

No Rest for a Recruit

Constable Robert MacGregor of the North-West Mounted Police was woken up by a splash of liquid mud on the end of his nose. Sleepily he brushed the mud away and settled deeper inside his blankets.

As junior recruit in his barrack room, Rob rated the worst positioned bed, the one right under the biggest leak in the roof. Not that his barrack-mates were much better off. Fort Macleod was as new as a building could be. It had been built by the Mounties themselves a few months earlier to provide shelter before winter came down. Unfortunately it had been built in some haste, and with rather more enthusiasm than skill. The roof leaked, the floors were damp and cold winds whistled icily through the many chinks in the log walls.

Still, thought Rob, he couldn't really grumble, since he had only himself to blame for his present position. Rob had gone to a lot of trouble to join the Mounties. He'd arrived too late to sign up with the rest of the recruits, and had accompanied them on their epic march west ostensibly as driver of one of the supply wagons. In reality he had been working as an undercover agent for Assistant Commissioner Macleod, now in command of the Fort. Rob had been instrumental in finding Fort Whoop-Up, secret hideout of the whisky traders, and had been allowed to join the Mounties as his reward.*

Now, as the morning bugle rang out, Rob wondered if becoming a Mountie had been such a good idea after all. The door of the barrack room was thrown open and Troop Sergeant Reilly appeared, immaculate and gleaming despite the early hour. It was rumoured amongst the recruits that Reilly didn't actually go to sleep; he just stood to attention all night, waiting for the morning bugle and the chance to start chasing them about again.

'Up with you, me lovely lads,' roared Reilly. 'You there, Constable MacGregor, you were the last in the Force, so be first out of bed!'

Rob groaned inwardly as he jumped out of bed and grabbed for his clothes. Rob's late arrival in the Force meant he'd missed training with the other recruits and Sergeant Reilly never let him forget it. He had put Rob in the special 'awkward squad', composed of recruits who were clumsy enough to need extra training. As he scrambled into his uniform Rob braced himself for the inevitable next remark. 'You may be the Commissioner's little pet, MacGregor, but that cuts no ice with me!'

By this, Reilly meant that Rob had joined the Force under the direct sponsorship of the Assistant Commissioner. Macleod had persuaded Commissioner French to bend the rules a little after Rob's services in helping to catch the whisky traders. Rob bitterly resented the way the Sergeant harped on this point. True enough, Macleod had got Rob into the Force, but he'd shown him no favours since then, nor had

* Told in *The Mounties—the Great March West.*

Rob expected any. He didn't want to be treated any better than anybody else, but he didn't see why he should be treated any worse.

In a mood of grim resignation, Rob began the tough daily routine. A hurried wash in the primitive washroom, first breaking the ice on the water jug. Over to the stables for an hour spent 'mucking out', and grooming his horse 'Brownie'. Then, at last, over to the Constables' Mess for breakfast.

Rob sat between his two friends, Fred Denbow and Henri Dubois. For a while everyone was too busy eating to talk much. Breakfast consisted of tea, bread and slices of tough, cold beef, and Rob munched away in gloomy silence. Fred gave him a sympathetic glance. 'How is it going, Rob?'

Rob grunted. 'Well enough. I just wish Reilly would leave me alone.'

Henri chuckled. 'The penalty of distinction, *mon ami*. The good Sergeant knows that after your glorious entry into our ranks they will soon make you Commissioner! He is simply jealous of your coming glory.'

Rob grinned in spite of himself, and drained the last of his strong sweet tea. 'Well, I'd best be off. I'm on riding instruction—under guess who?'

The riding instruction, or 'Ride' as it was called, took place on the bare windy plain outside the Fort. The 'awkward squad' jogged round Sergeant Reilly in a circle. They were riding bareback, and just to make things more difficult, with their arms folded on their chests.

Rob had been riding horses since boyhood, and had

always thought himself reasonably competent. But his idea of riding and Sergeant Reilly's were very different. Reilly had served in the Army back in England. He was determined his men should attain the same high standard as an English Cavalry regiment. Rob's thigh-muscles ached, and he'd never realised before how sharp and bony was the ridge of a horse's spine. Brownie stumbled awkwardly on the icy ground and Rob felt himself slipping sideways. Desperately he tightened the grip of his knees, but it was too late. He keeled over sideways and thudded to the iron-hard ground with a thump that knocked the breath from his body. Brownie, well-used to the Ride by now, went on placidly trotting round the circle without him.

As Rob struggled to sit up he saw Sergeant Reilly towering above him. 'Who ordered you to dismount, Constable MacGregor?'

Rob climbed painfully to his feet. 'No one, Sergeant. I just fell.'

'This is the *Mounted* Police, Constable MacGregor. You are not *allowed* to fall!'

Rob clenched his jaw, climbed back on his horse, and without waiting for orders went on jogging round the circle.

Riding practice went on until mid-day stables. Then came lunch. This was much like breakfast, except that the beef was replaced by buffalo meat, and accompanied with flapjacks. These were a kind of pancake as tough and leathery as the meat. It was rumoured that because of the absence of butter the cooks fried them in axle grease. As he chewed away doggedly Rob could well believe it.

After lunch it was back outside the Fort again for weapons practice. Hidden targets were set up and Rob and the rest of the awkward squad rode to a point just a mile away. On the word of command they rode at full gallop towards the targets. When the targets appeared they had to dismount, fire, reload their single-shot carbines, remount and gallop on. The targets appeared and disappeared four times in the mile ride, and since they stayed up for just one minute, it was hard enough to get off a shot, let alone score a hit. Rob, who was a naturally good marksman, managed to knock up a pretty good score, which cheered him considerably.

Rifle practice was followed by revolver practice, this time at twenty-five yards. Firing on foot, firing when mounted, firing at a walk, firing at full gallop.

By the end of the afternoon Rob's shoulder ached from the bruising recoil of the butt of his Snider–Enfield carbine, and his wrist from the weight of the heavy Adams ·45 Revolver.

Then, mercifully, it was time for tea. This meal was just what its name implied, mugs of tea with chunks of dry bread. Then evening stables, with the horses to be groomed, fed and settled for the night. At the end of the day Rob staggered back to his barrack-room and collapsed on the bed with a thankful groan.

Fred and Henri were sitting on their beds cleaning their kit. They'd spent a day hauling water from the nearby creek, and though they'd worked hard enough, they weren't nearly as exhausted as Rob. Fred grinned sympathetically.

'Feeling the pace, old chap?'

Rob stretched and relaxed his aching muscles. 'You might say that. All right for you two, trotting up and down with your little water cart all day.'

Henri shrugged. 'Privilege of long service,' he said airily. Fred and Henri had been in the Mounties about three months longer than Rob.

Rob yawned. 'All right, Henri, you can stop coming the old soldier. I'm not moving off this bed till——'

'Lazing about again, Constable MacGregor?' The roomful of constables scrambled to their feet as Sergeant Reilly marched into the barrack room. Rob got up too, but he took his time. He'd had quite enough of being bustled about for one day.

The Sergeant marched up to Rob's bed. 'Well, it so happens there's a few extra fatigues going, and I think I see a volunteer.'

Rob stiffened in anger, and his big bony fists clenched at his sides.

'Now see here, Sergeant Reilly——'

Fred suddenly spoke, 'Steady, Rob!' and Rob's mouth snapped shut. Fred and Henri looked at him warningly. Despite his usually placid nature, Rob had quite a temper, and it would be fatal for him to lose it now. Disobeying a Sergeant was bad enough, but walloping one . . .

Sergeant Reilly looked at the silent angry figure before him with malicious enjoyment. 'Well, *Constable* MacGregor, you're on fatigues. Anything to say?'

Rob took a deep breath. Before he could reply, a

voice spoke from the doorway behind him. 'Maybe he don't, but I do.'

Sergeant Reilly spun round in outraged surprise. A small, dark man in shabby buckskins was leaning casually against the door post. The black Indian eyes in his heavily moustached face were quietly amused. The Sergeant snorted. 'Oh it's you, Potts. What do *you* want?'

Jerry Potts was a half-breed scout who had been working for the Mounties since the Force was formed. Son of a Scottish trapper and a Blood Indian squaw, he had an unparalleled knowledge of the North-West country and the ways of the Indian tribes. Jerry looked up at the big Sergeant quite unimpressed. '*I* want Constable MacGregor. Leastways, Commissioner Macleod wants him. You got any objections?'

Reilly did his best to put a good face on things. 'All right, MacGregor, smarten yourself up and report to the Commissioner right away.' He turned back to Jerry. 'No need for you to hang about, Potts, you've delivered your message.'

Jerry didn't move from his lounging position. 'You don't give me orders, Sergeant. I go where I like, do what I damn please.' The big Sergeant took a step forward, then paused. For all his small size and mild manner, Jerry Potts was a dangerous man to cross. He had a reputation as a gunfighter, and was rumoured to have killed a number of men. Rob had seen Jerry in action, and could easily believe in the stories. The Sergeant opened his mouth, closed it again and marched angrily out of the room.

A hum of applause went up as soon as he was out of

earshot. Evans, a gloomy Welsh Constable, was particularly enthusiastic.

'You tell him, Jerry. Disgraceful it is the way he goes on at us.'

Jerry shrugged, but said nothing. He never wasted words. Despite the lack of encouragement, Evans continued his complaints. 'Fair disgusting the way we're treated. No pay since we joined, lousy food, no proper equipment...' He held up a worn and shabby pair of boots. 'Look at *them*, now. Worn through on the March, and nothing in the stores to replace them.'

There were murmurs of agreement throughout the room. Brushing down his uniform, Rob looked at Evans with disfavour. The man was a born moaner, always grumbling about something. But unfortunately, many of his complaints were true. Conditions *were* bad at Fort Macleod, though considering how quickly the Force had been assembled and sent to the North-West, it was surprising they were no worse. Most of the men contented themselves with a good grumble, knowing things would eventually improve. But the grumbles had been a lot more frequent of late.

Rob stood up, straightened his tunic and reached for his hat. 'I'm not complaining,' he said gruffly. 'I just don't like being picked on. Come on, Jerry.'

As they walked across the barrack square, passing the big central flagpost and the low square shape of the powder magazine, Rob paused by the two field guns. 'Any idea what it's about, Jerry? Macleod tell you?'

At Rob's appealing look, Jerry relented enough to

24

add, 'Maybe we go little trip.' And not another word would he say until they entered Macleod's office.

Assistant Commissioner James Farquarson Macleod, Commanding Officer of the Fort bearing his name, was a bearded giant of a man whose deep booming voice could strike terror into the toughest old soldier. He was busily composing yet another vitriolic cable to Government headquarters in Ottowa complaining about the continued non-arrival of vital stores and the money to pay his men. If that didn't work, he thought, fiercely twisting his moustache, he'd go to Ottowa himself to shake the money and supplies out of them. He threw the cable down as Rob and Jerry entered. Rob came to attention before his desk. 'All right, Constable, at ease.' Macleod looked at the tall, brawny figure in the scarlet tunic, remembering the gangling farm boy who'd pleaded to be allowed to join the Force just six months ago. Rob had filled out now, his long bony face was weathered, and there was a determined set to the stubborn jaw. Boys turned to men fast in the Mounties—if they lasted the course. He wondered how Rob was doing. 'Well, boy,' he rumbled, 'how does life in the Mounted Police suit you? Any complaints?'

Rob thought of the grindingly hard recruit training, the monotonous food, the damp, draughty barracks and, worst of all, the constant harrying of Sergeant Reilly. 'No, sir. Everything's just fine.'

Macleod smiled. 'I see you've learned the soldier's motto. Never explain, never complain. Let me put it another way—do you think you could bear to be separated from Sergeant Reilly for a while?'

'I could bear it fine, sir.'

Macleod waved a hand. 'Sit down, both of you.' Rob perched uneasily on a hard wooden chair, and Jerry Potts dropped cat-like to the floor, where he crouched, Indian-fashion. Macleod produced a long cigar from a nearly empty box, lit it and puffed out a cloud of blue smoke. 'You'll be aware I've had visits from quite a few of the Indian chiefs?'

Even since the building of the Fort there had been a steady trickle of curious Indian visitors. Macleod received them formally, showed them round, smoked the pipe of peace with them. Then, with Jerry acting as interpreter, he delivered his set speech, assuring them the Police had come to bring law and order, that white men and Indians would be treated with equal fairness. The Indians listened impassively, then went on their way with gifts of clothes and tobacco.

'Unfortunately,' Macleod went on, 'the one visitor I hoped for has not arrived. I refer to Chief Crowfoot.'

Rob could understand Macleod's concern. Crowfoot was by far the greatest of the Indian chiefs, ruling a whole group of different tribes, a loose alliance called the Blackfoot Federation. Thousands of fierce warriors rode at his command, a force big enough to wipe out the Mounties with ease should Crowfoot prove hostile.

Macleod took another puff at his cigar. 'Now Jerry here has a theory about the Chief's non-appearance.'

Jerry spoke, 'Crowfoot big Chief. Like King or Emperor. Damn proud. He not come unless you ask.'

'I think Jerry's probably right,' said Macleod.

'Crowfoot hasn't come because he hasn't been invited. So I propose to send him a formal invitation!'

Rob felt he was expected to say something. 'Will you send a detachment out, sir?'

'I considered that. But we're still not too sure how Crowfoot feels about us. A party of armed men, however small, might be seen as provocation. But *one* man—plus of course a suitable guide ... No one could call that an invasion, could they?' Macleod sat back in his chair with the satisfied air of a master-diplomat.

Jerry Potts' eyes widened. 'You going to send just *one* policeman into Blackfoot country? Indians think either you mad or you got damn big medicine!'

'Precisely! Well, Constable MacGregor? Since you've already met Chief Crowfoot ...'

Rob looked at him. 'I take it you're wanting me to deliver this invitation, sir?'

'That's right. You and Potts will leave for Blackfoot country tomorrow morning.'

Rob was determined to get things quite clear.

'Just the two of us, sir?'

'Just the two of you.'

2

'I say kill the Red Coats!'

A few days later, Fort Macleod far behind them, Rob
and Jerry were riding across the great plains through
Blackfoot country. The weather was sunny but cold,
the air crisp and clear. Although spring was coming
the plains were still partly covered with snow. The
two riders were bundled up in winter kit, coats, hats,
and mittens all of fur.

Rob was riding Brownie, while Jerry rode a wiry
Indian pony. So far, they'd been lucky with the
weather. The snow held off and they made good time,
the hard ground ringing beneath the horses' feet.

Rob's mood was a mixture of doubt and exhil-
aration. It was wonderful to be free, to be away from
the confinement and discipline of the Fort. But he
was well aware that every day's ride took them deeper
into danger, further from any possible help. The
Blackfoot warriors ruled supreme in this land. Should
they prove hostile, Rob and Jerry wouldn't have a
chance.

Rob had once met Chief Crowfoot at the time
when he was working undercover for Macleod. He
had been rescued by the Blackfoot from death at the
hands of their enemies the Sioux, and had spent many
days in Crowfoot's village. This was obviously why
Rob had been selected for the mission. But he kept
remembering that in those days he hadn't been a

Mountie. Crowfoot had made it clear that his attitude towards the red-coated intruders into his territory was by no means welcoming. Already some of the Chief's advisers were telling him the red coat soldiers had come to steal his lands and kill his people, just as the hated 'Long Knives', the U.S. Cavalry, were doing in America. And if Crowfoot had been suspicious when the Mounties first arrived, how would he feel now they were well established in his territory, building forts and clearly intending to stay?

By Rob's request, Jerry made their last camp in a dry ravine, just a few hours' ride from Crowfoot's village. So far they had seen no Indians, though that didn't mean the Blackfoot had not seen them.

After breakfast of coffee, pemmican (a kind of tough dried meat) and flapjacks, Rob used the campfire to boil up more water in his billycan. Watched by an astonished Jerry he washed and shaved. Then he cleaned up his Mountie uniform, polished his boots and belt, and carefully brushed down trousers and tunic.

Huddled in his furs, Jerry grunted, 'We having parade maybe?'

Rob went on with his spit and polish, grooming Brownie and even polishing the saddle and harness. 'You know what Indians do for a big occasion, Jerry. They put on their best robes to make good medicine. Well, this uniform is *my* medicine.'

Jerry grunted and set about striking camp. 'We better hope it works.'

Soon they were cantering towards the Blackfoot camp, Rob in the lead. He had left off his winter furs and his red tunic looked startlingly bright against the snow.

Although the plains Indians were great warriors, they seldom participated in the duller parts of military duties. Few Indian villages bothered to post sentries, and it was purely chance that Rob was spotted by a solitary brave fishing in the river that bordered the camp. Unfortunately this particular warrior was very young and highly excitable. As soon as he saw the scarlet tunic he ran wildly into the village, shouting that the red coat soldiers were coming to attack. Instantly the camp erupted into life, warriors grabbing weapons vaulted on to their horses, preparing to stand off the attack.

In Chief Crowfoot's big lodge, one of his sub-chiefs turned towards him in angry excitement. 'Now perhaps the Chief will listen to my voice. Did I not say from the first that the soldiers would come to attack us and steal our lands? I say kill the Red Coats!'

Crowfoot said nothing. Slowly, with the dignity befitting a Chief, he strode from his tent.

As Rob and Jerry rode down towards the river they saw a mob of armed warriors galloping furiously from the camp, yelling and waving their weapons, prepared to hurl themselves on the enemy.

When they realised that the enemy consisted of just two men, they reined to a halt with almost comical suddenness.

Rob and Jerry rode steadily forward, and the astonished warriors drew aside to let them pass. As the Indians looked closer, they began murmuring to each other in surprise. Jerry was an old friend of the Blackfoot, and many of them also recognised Rob.

'It is Mas-gwa-ah-sid,' they shouted. Jerry looked at Rob, who winced and almost blushed. Mas-gwa-ah-sid, or Bear Paw, was his Indian name, given after he had defeated an armed warrior with his bare fists. It had amused the Indians to say that a blow from Rob's fist was like the mighty swipe of the paw of an angry bear.

Followed by the crowd, Rob rode slowly through the camp and reined in his horse outside Crowfoot's lodge. The Chief stood waiting, surrounded by his sub-chiefs. Rob raised his hand in a formal salute.

Crowfoot returned the greeting. 'Tell us, Mas-gwa-ah-sid, do you come in peace or war?'

Rob was too astonished to reply. Solemnly Crowfoot went on, 'The hearts of my warriors are timid. They fear that you come to attack them. Calm their fears and say that you will do them no harm.'

A roar of guttural laughter swept through the excited crowd, and they began shoving and pushing each other, mocking their own alarm. Rob saw that while some of the chiefs around Crowfoot joined in the laughter, others stood silent and angry. He guessed the Mounties still had their enemies in the Blackfoot camp.

Jerry disappeared to visit friends in the village. Crowfoot's English was good, so Rob had no need of an interpreter. Soon he was sitting in Crowfoot's tepee, puffing awkwardly at the long pipe of peace. He passed the long, ceremonial pipe back to Crowfoot, who took a solemn puff and put it aside. 'There is great cunning in the mind of your Chief. Instead of many red coat soldiers he sends but one, and that one a friend.'

Rob delivered Macleod's invitation to visit him at the Fort, and Crowfoot listened without comment. When Rob had finished the Chief spoke, 'My heart is glad at this message from your Chief. I have much curiosity to see the Fort and the red coat soldiers. Truly they must be mighty warriors if but one of their number dares to invade the territory of the Blackfoot.' Rob grinned in appreciation of the Chief's deadpan joke. More seriously the Chief went on. 'Yet I do not know if I *should* come. A Chief is not free as are other men. Always he must consider what is best for his people. In this matter of the red coat soldiers, my people speak with many voices. Some say they come to make us slaves, that we should kill them now and burn their Forts. Yet you tell me that only the evil need fear them, and my heart wishes to believe your words.'

'My words are true,' said Rob quietly. 'Have we not driven out the whisky traders, closed down Fort Whoop-Up?'

'It is true that the Fort is no more. Yet the whisky traders still bring firewater to corrupt my people.'

Rob wasn't surprised to hear that whisky trading still continued. The Mounties had closed the whisky forts, and broken up the big American-financed ring, but it was probable that much of the trade had only gone underground. There would be plenty of independent traders ready to risk prosecution for a chance at huge profits.

Rob said confidently. '*All* the whisky traders will be caught and punished, I promise you. It's just a matter of time.

'And the murderers of our brothers the Assiniboine, those who shot down women and children in the Cypress Hills? Much time has already passed, yet still they are free, across the medicine line. How long before *they* are punished?'

Rob found it hard to answer. It was true that nearly two years had passed since the Cypress Hills massacre, and the killers were still unpunished. He made the best reply he could.

'We both know there has been no law in this land for many years. Whisky traders, robbers, murderers, all kinds of criminals white *and* Indian, have done as they pleased. Well, now the Police are here and that's all going to change. But it won't happen overnight. It'll take months, maybe years to bring the law to the North-West. *But it will be done* ... if you give us your trust and your help.'

Crowfoot was silent for a moment. Then he said, 'I will consider your words, and discuss them with my chiefs.' It was obvious that the audience was at an end, and Rob stood up and left the tepee.

Later, over a meal of buffalo steak, Rob discussed the meeting with Jerry Potts. 'Indian got long memory,' said Jerry. 'Never break promise, expect same from you. You say you stop whisky traders, catch Indian killers, you better do it.'

Rob chewed on the succulent buffalo steak. He was eating better in the Indian camp than he ever did at the Fort. 'I only hope we can, Jerry. I think Crowfoot

would like to be friendly, but he's being very cautious.'

Jerry grunted. 'Crowfoot great chief. Where he
goes, rest follow.'

'He says the Cypress Hills killers are over the
American border.'

Jerry took a swig of his beer. 'Why not? In
America, killing Indians don't make you criminal,
make you hero.'

Rob said nothing. But he determined that the
matter of the Cypress Hills massacre would figure
very largely in his report to Macleod.

Later that day the Chief sent for Rob to give his
decision. Rob was tense as he entered the big tepee.
Soon he would know whether he had succeeded or
failed in his mission. Crowfoot came to the point at
once. 'Tell your Chief I will come to the Fort.'

Rob let out a sigh of relief. 'He'll be as glad to hear
it as I am. With your permission, I'll start back at
once with the news.'

'You are welcome to stay with us longer. My son
Red Crow will return soon from his hunting. His
heart will be sad if he does not see you.'

Rob had become good friends with the Chief's
young son during his previous visit to the camp, but
he shook his head regretfully. 'My orders were to
return at once. But I'd very much like to see Red
Crow again. Maybe he could come to the Fort with
you?'

Crowfoot nodded gravely. 'Your Chief is well
served. We shall meet at the Fort.'

Soon Rob and Jerry were on the move again, riding

back towards Fort Macleod. Rob had plenty to think about on the ride. It was clear that although Crowfoot wasn't actively hostile to the Mounted Police, he would need a lot of convincing before he abandoned his attitude of cautious neutrality. It was clear too that some of the Chief's councillors were hostile, and would use every opportunity to try to bring Chief Crowfoot round to their way of thinking. Much would depend on the coming meeting between Crowfoot and Macleod.

They made good time on the journey back. Despite Jerry's gloomy prophecies of snow, the crisp clear weather continued. As their journey neared its end, Rob found himself looking forward to sleeping indoors again. After a succession of days in the saddle and nights in the open, even his hard bed in the draughty barrack room of Fort Macleod began to look welcoming.

He said as much as they packed up camp after their last night on the trail. Jerry reckoned they should reach the Fort late that afternoon. The little scout shrugged. 'Easy trip this. Lucky we don't get blizzard.'

Rob fastened his saddle-bag and mounted Brownie. 'Well it's been tough enough for me—and I can do without your blizzard, thanks.'

Jerry glanced at the sky. 'Blizzard come, you see.'

Rob was lost in thought as they rode along. Mentally he was preparing his report to Macleod. There must be *something* they could do about finding the Cypress Hills killers, though it wouldn't be easy now the men were back on American soil ... Jerry's voice interrupted his thoughts. 'Someone on trail.'

Jerry was standing up in his stirrups, shading his eyes with his hand. Rob peered in the same direction and could just make out a distant figure. It seemed to be on foot and was weaving to and fro aimlessly. 'What do you think it is? Somebody hurt?'

Jerry touched spurs to his pony's flanks. 'Mebbe. We go see.'

As they rode closer, Rob saw that the man on the trail was an Indian, a muscular giant of a man. Despite the cold, he was stripped to breech-clout and moccasins and, more surprising still, he seemed to be completely unarmed. He was staggering along, weaving backwards and forwards as if in a daze.

Jerry Potts rode up to the Indian, blocking his way with the pony. He called out something in one of the Indian languages. At first the huge Indian just stared dully, not seeming to understand. Then as Jerry spoke again the Indian gave a roar of rage, reached up and dragged him from his saddle. Jerry crashed to the ground and the Indian hurled his enormous bulk on top of him, massive hands reaching out.

Rob dived from his saddle, and landed on top of the struggling pile. He locked an arm round the Indian's throat and managed to drag him away. As Jerry rolled clear, the Indian threw off Rob's grip with ease and jumped on *him*, bearing him to the ground. As he struggled to keep the enormous hands from his throat, Rob felt like a small child in the grip of a large and angry adult. Over his attacker's shoulder he caught a glimpse of Jerry. The scout had drawn his Colt and was obviously waiting for the chance of a clear shot. Rob just had time to yell, 'Jerry, don't shoot!' before the Indian's hands choked off his voice. Jerry looked puzzled, but instead of firing the revolver he slammed the barrel to the side of the Indian's head. The big warrior jerked and went limp, leaving Rob still pinned to the ground by his weight.

Panting for breath Rob wriggled from beneath him and struggled to his feet. 'What did you say to upset him, Jerry?' he gasped reproachfully.

Jerry shot him an indignant look. 'Say nothing. Ask if he in trouble, need help.'

'Then why did he set about us? Is he mad?'

Jerry rolled the unconscious warrior on his back, leaned over him cautiously and sniffed. 'Not mad. Drunk. Same thing for Indian.' He caught his horse and prepared to mount. 'Come on. We go before he wake up.'

Rob shook his head. 'No. When he wakes up I want to find out how he got so drunk in the first place.'

The Indian was surprisingly docile when he finally came round. They lit a small fire and made camp, boiling up quantities of black coffee to help sober him up. Wrapped in one of their blankets the crestfallen giant crouched shivering over the fire, sadly answering Jerry's questions in a deep, rumbling voice. When the questioning was finished Jerry looked up at Rob. 'He Cree Indian. Say his name Two Bulls.'

Rob looked at the huge form of the Indian. 'I can see why. What happened to him?'

'He go to 'nother village, buy horses. On way back

meet whisky traders. Two wagons, four men. Trade horses for whisky. Drink whisky, plenty drunk. Trade for more whisky—clothes, gun, everything. Don't remember no more.' Jerry sniffed disgustedly. 'Damn fool Indian.'

'When did this happen—and where?'

Jerry fired a few more questions at the Indian, listened to his replies and said, 'Late last night. Place called Pine Bluff, not far away.'

'Do you know where it is?'

'Sure I know.'

Rob emptied the coffee-pot, packed it away and started stamping out the little fire.

'Come on then, Jerry. Oh, and tell our friend he's coming with us.'

Jerry looked back in astonishment. He nodded towards the Indian, still huddled in his blanket. 'Why you take him back to Fort? Macleod don't want drunk Indian.'

'We're not going to the Fort, not yet anyway. We're going to Pine Bluff to arrest some whisky traders.'

3

'You're under arrest'

Jerry looked unbelievingly at Rob. 'You, me and one drunk Indian? We going to capture two wagon-loads full of whisky traders?'

'Why not? We'll have the advantage of surprise.'

'We get surprise. Surprised to death, mebbe. Anyway, Macleod say go straight back to Fort. We tell him, he send patrol.'

'And by the time we get back to the Fort, tell Macleod what happened, and he gets a patrol under way, the whisky traders could be miles away. We've got to get them ourselves.'

It took quite a while to convince Jerry, then even longer to convince Two Bulls. Finally Rob told Jerry to offer him a choice. Imprisonment for attacking a Policeman, or a chance to get his goods back and his revenge on the men who had cheated him. Two Bulls decided to come with them.

At last they were under way, Two Bulls trotting beside the horses. It took them the rest of the day to reach Pine Bluffs, and it was growing dark as they stood looking at the traces of a camp fire. 'See? Whisky traders gone,' said Jerry, adding hopefully, 'we go back to Fort now?'

'Not on your life. We camp here tonight, follow their tracks in the morning.' Rob slapped Jerry on the shoulder. 'They say you can track a grasshopper across these plains. Don't tell me you can't follow two loaded wagons?'

'I follow all right,' said Jerry gloomily. 'What happens when we find them?'

Rob grinned. 'Don't worry. I'll think of something.'

Next morning they set off on the track of the whisky traders. The trail was easy to follow and they moved slowly and carefully. Rob wanted to be sure he saw the whisky traders before they saw him. The beginning of a plan was forming in his mind.

It was late afternoon by the time they caught up with their quarry. Jerry reined in his horse at the top of a rise and pointed. 'There!' Down below, where the trail forded a narrow creek bordered with poplar trees, two wagons were standing beneath the trees. A couple of ponies were tethered to the rear wagon. Evidently the whisky traders had decided to make an early camp. Two men were at work unhitching the horses. Two more were setting up camp. Rob studied the ground for a moment. 'Couldn't be better. Now then, Jerry, you see those trees over there...'

A few minutes later Rob was riding slowly towards the whisky traders' camp. He was wrapped in a blanket and slumped low in his saddle.

In front of him rode Two Bulls on Jerry's pony. Rob tried to keep the big Indian between himself and the eyeline of the men in the camp. His idea was to pass for an Indian as long as possible.

The men round the wagons looked up with no particular interest or alarm as two blanket-wrapped figures jogged slowly towards them. As Rob had hoped, the genuineness of the first figure drew attention away from the second.

The leader of the traders, a thin swarthy man with a straggly moustache, looked up from his campfire as the two riders approached. 'Hey, ain't that the big Indian we traded with a while back? He must be coming back for more.'

His companion nodded. 'Seems like he's found himself another horse and blanket. Brought a friend with him too ...'

The swarthy man looked more closely at the second rider. 'Just hold on now, that ain't no Indian. Hey, mister, who——'

Before he could finish, Rob touched spurs to Brownie and overtook the Indian, reining to a halt in front of the two men. He flung back the blanket to reveal the scarlet of his tunic. The whisky traders stared at him. It was a moment before the leader recovered enough to speak. 'Who the blazes are you, mister?' he asked in genuine astonishment. So recently had the Police come to the North-West that many of the inhabitants had never even seen a Mountie.

Rob was trembling with excitement, but he tried to make his voice sound calm and assured. 'I'm a Constable in the North-West Mounted Police. You're under arrest for whisky trading.' Quite a moment, he thought. My first arrest. Just so long as it isn't my last ...

The expression of amazement on the swarthy man's face was almost comical. Then white teeth flashed beneath his moustache in a sudden grin. 'Hey, boys, it's one of them new-fangled Mounties. Come to take us in all by his-self!'

The second man joined in the joke. 'Don't forget the Indian, boss. Maybe he's a Mountie too!'

Rob waited till the laughter died down. His voice was deadly serious. 'You're all under arrest. I'm ordering you to throw down your guns.'

All at once the atmosphere changed. In a voice equally serious the swarthy man said, 'You want these guns, you'll have to take them.' The men by the horses, sensing something was wrong, started moving towards them.

Rob surveyed the little group. All four looked tough and dangerous. They wore revolvers, and had rifles close by. Rob made no move to draw his own. The Mountie holster wasn't made for a fast draw, and even if he got the gun out in time, he couldn't hope to outshoot four men.

The leader rasped a hand across his stubbly chin. 'Maybe you'd better just hand over *your* gun...' To reinforce his words, he reached for the Winchester propped against a wagon wheel.

A shot rang out in the clear cold air. The bullet hit the iron rim of the wagon wheel and ricocheted away with a shrill whining sound. The whisky trader dropped the rifle and jumped back. As the other man reached for his revolver, a shot ripped through the canvas of the wagon close behind him. The man dropped his hand, and stood very still.

Rob said, 'Your camp is surrounded by my men. *Now let me have those guns.*'

Almost in a daze the whisky traders unbuckled

their gunbelts and let them drop. Rob drew his own revolver and cocked it. 'Now, move away from them. Bunch up over there. And don't move too close to your rifles.'

The four men obediently moved back. Rob nodded to Two Bulls, hoping he would remember Jerry's instructions. The Indian jumped down from his pony and began collecting up rifles and pistols, piling them in a heap at Rob's feet. One of the traders seemed reluctant to give up his gun, so Two Bulls took it, picked him up and threw him out of the way. Everyone co-operated after that.

Rob raised his own revolver and fired in the air. A few minutes later Jerry Potts strolled out of the trees, his rifle covering the small group. The swarthy whisky trader looked up at Rob. 'Where's the rest of your men?'

'He's them,' said Rob succinctly. 'But don't get any ideas. That's Jerry Potts.'

The whisky trader sighed, letting his shoulders slump. Obviously he had heard of Jerry. 'O.K., Mountie, you got us. There won't be no trouble.'

While Jerry guarded the prisoners, Rob made a quick search of the wagons. One was loaded with whisky, the other with buffalo skins and furs, the proceeds of successful trading.

Two Bulls pointed eagerly to the tethered ponies, and grabbed an armful of the furs. Rob reached up and patted him on the shoulder. 'You'll get them all back. You've earned them.'

It occurred to Rob that perhaps he'd stumbled on a method of tracking down the whisky traders. Quite a few Indians were eager to trade for whisky, but when the firewater was gone they were left with nothing but a sore head and a feeling of resentment. If they could be persuaded to come to the Mounties ... He explained the idea to Jerry, who chuckled appreciatively. 'Damn right. Trade for whisky. Get drunk. Turn in traders, get furs back. Reward too, maybe. Good business for Indian—bad for them!' He jerked a thumb towards the prisoners. 'We go back to Fort now, eh? Nice little present for Macleod!'

Unaware of the treat in store for him, Commissioner Macleod sat hunched over the roaring stove in his headquarters. The stove top was glowing cherry red, but just a few feet away from it the corners of the room were icy cold. Macleod was sipping the end of his whisky and smoking one of his last cigars. Not that this worried him particularly. He was an old campaigner: he liked his luxuries when he could get them, but if he couldn't he was perfectly prepared to do without. What did worry him was the tale of woe being poured out by Inspector Jarvis, who sat in the chair on the other side of the stove.

Jarvis was a long, lean melancholy man with a face well suited to the telling of dismal stories. Macleod couldn't help feeling that Jarvis was enjoying himself. He knew this was unfair since Jarvis, a good conscientious officer, was genuinely worried, but it annoyed him just the same.

'Thing is, sir,' Jarvis was saying, 'it's not only the trouble-makers now. The good men are beginning to grumble too. We could soon be faced with something like a mutiny.'

Macleod spread his big hands out to the warmth of the stove, and gazed deep into the flames.

'Scarcely surprising, is it? You take a scratch force of men, hurriedly organised, hurriedly recruited. A few ex-soldiers, the rest farm-boys, drug-store clerks, schoolteachers, shop-assistants, miners, anything and everything as long as they're young and fit. You force-march them a thousand miles across unknown country and dump them down to spend winter in a ricketty fort surrounded by thousands of hostile Indians. Then, just in case anyone thinks you're spoiling 'em, you arrange to keep them short of food, clothes and supplies. And just to add the finishing touch, you don't pay them a single damned dollar!'

Jarvis stared in astonishment at the Commissioner. An unimaginative man himself, Jarvis hadn't realised how deeply Macleod felt the troubles of his men.

Macleod went on, 'I've sent a rider to Fort Benton to send a message for transmission to Ottawa by the U.S. Army Telegraph. I've warned the Government in the strongest terms. We need supplies, food, and above all *money*! I just hope they have the sense to listen.' He raked moodily at the stove. 'And to top it all, Constable MacGregor and Jerry Potts are long overdue.'

Tactfully Jarvis said nothing. He'd always been opposed to the idea of sending one inexperienced constable, and one scout, on such a dangerous mission. Now it seemed events had proved him right. Jarvis privately thought that Jerry Potts and Mac-

Gregor's scalps were probably decorating some Blackfoot lodge, though he didn't dare say so to Macleod.

The Commissioner rose and stretched. 'Well, there's nothing we can do but hang on.' He threw the butt of his cigar into the flames. 'You know, Jarvis, it's the inactivity that's causing all the trouble. On the march, when we were in real danger, the men were magnificent. Best thing for us all right now would be an Indian attack. Pull everyone together splendidly!'

Jarvis rose too, not entirely sure if Macleod was joking. Suddenly the door was thrown open. An excited constable rushed in, forgetting to salute in his haste. 'Message from the lookout sir. Large party of Indians heading for the Fort. They've already opened fire!'

Jarvis looked at the Commissioner. 'Well, sir, it seems you have your wish!'

Moments later, Macleod and Jarvis were standing on the lookout platform. Macleod had binoculars to his eyes. 'It's a big party all right. Two or three hundred braves, maybe more.' He lowered the binoculars and turned to the excited group around him.

'Very well, gentlemen, I want all men at their posts, the field guns loaded and manned. And remember no one is to fire until I personally give the order. Sentry, sound the call to arms!'

Rob and Jerry, with their prisoners, were on the far side of the hill overlooking the Fort when they heard the bugles. Rob looked up in alarm. 'There's something happening at the Fort. Jerry, you and Two Bulls hold the prisoners here while I take a look.'

Before Jerry could reply, Rob was spurring his horse up the hill. He reined in at the top and looked down. Below him stood the Fort, red coated figures scurrying about on the walls. Beyond, and still some way off on the plains was a huge crowd of Indians. Rob could see little knots of braves ahead of the main body, riding to and fro firing shots in the air. Rob shaded his eyes with his hand. Surely he recognised that figure in the forefront of the main group ... It was Chief Crowfoot.

Rob looked from the Indians to the Fort and back again. With a sudden shock he realised what was happening. Crowfoot must have set off for the Fort soon after Rob and Jerry. And because of their detour to chase the whisky traders, he had arrived before them!

Since Rob had failed to return, there was a fair chance that the Mounties would assume the Indians to be hostile. Rob touched spurs to Brownie's flanks and rode at top speed down the steep trail to the Fort.

On the lookout platform, Jarvis pointed towards the two field-guns. They had been manhandled to a position where they commanded the main gates. 'Shall we open the gates and give 'em a few rounds, sir? They're not used to artillery, it'll maybe scare them off.'

Macleod shook his head. 'I won't open fire till I'm sure.'

'The enemy are already shooting at *us*, sir.' From the distance could be heard the crack of rifle shots.

'They're shooting,' said Macleod calmly, 'but not

necessarily at us—not unless they're remarkably bad shots. We'll wait.'

Rob rode up to the rear gate of the Fort and hammered on it with all his might. A nervous sentry poked his head over the stockade, covering him with his rifle. 'It's me, MacGregor,' yelled Rob. 'Open up and let me in!'

Once inside Rob jumped down from his horse.

'Where's Macleod?' The man pointed and Rob saw the burly figure of the Commissioner on the lookout platform. He ran across the compound, dashed up the steps and arrived panting in front of Macleod, barely remembering to salute. The Commissioner said cheerfully, 'Ah, there you are, Constable MacGregor! Can you explain what's going on out there?' He pointed over the stockade to the approaching Indians, now very close.

'Yes I can, sir. That's Chief Crowfoot and his people. He accepted your invitation to visit the Fort.'

'Then why didn't you return as ordered to report the fact?'

'We were delayed by some whisky traders, sir. Jerry's bringing them in now.' Rob waved his hand dismissively. 'I'll explain all that later. The important thing is, Crowfoot *must* be given a friendly welcome. If anyone opens fire he'll think your invitation was a trap and we'll finish up with a massacre.'

Jarvis said obstinately. 'Then why are his warriors shooting at us?'

'That's just the young braves, sir. They're sort of showing off—it's like a parade, that's all.'

Jarvis wasn't convinced. 'If Crowfoot's friendly why

did he bring so many warriors? We didn't invite the whole tribe.'

'Crowfoot's a very important man, sir … Queen Victoria doesn't go out on her own either.'

Macleod's mouth twitched, but he growled. 'That will do, Constable MacGregor. You're *sure* those Indians are friendly?'

'I'd stake my life on it, sir.'

'That's exactly what you are doing, MacGregor—all our lives.'

Macleod came to a decision. Turning to face the compound he shouted, 'Listen to me, all of you. The Indians are friendly, I repeat, friendly. Inspectors, form your men into a guard of honour. Artillerymen, load with blank and prepare to fire salutes. Somebody fetch my horse. Constable MacGregor, come with me!'

The gates of the Fort were thrown open. The Indians heard the double boom of the field guns, and saw a line of scarlet coated horsemen trotting towards them, a burly bearded figure at its head. Assistant Commissioner Macleod was riding out to greet his guests.

4

Macleod's Justice

'This court is now in session!' Together with the other witnesses and spectators, Rob rose to his feet as Commissioner Macleod entered the room.

The 'courtroom' was the Officers' Mess, dressed up for the occasion. A trestle table had been set up against the end wall, with a Union Jack draped on the wall behind it. Next to the flag, a portrait of a severe-looking Queen Victoria added a touch of dignity to the occasion. In front of the table, benches had been set up for prisoners and witnesses. At the far end of the room was the 'public gallery', a roped-off area with seats for spectators. Among them sat Chief Crowfoot and a few of his chosen advisers.

It made an impressive enough scene, thought Rob, as he glanced round the improvised courtroom. Except for the clearly visible remains of the buffalo trail that ran across the dirt floor, it might have been the Old Bailey.

It was the third day of Chief Crowfoot's visit to the Fort, and so far things were going well. The Chief had been pleased by his elaborate reception, the honour guard of armed Mounties and the booming salutes from the field guns. It was lucky for everyone, thought Rob, that Crowfoot didn't realise how close he'd come to getting a very different reception. The Indians had pitched camp outside the Fort, a village springing up overnight. The arrival of the Indians and the capture of the whisky traders had provided a welcome distraction for the garrison, and morale at the Fort was better than it had been for some time. The Indians wandered round the Fort like curious children, and the Mounties were made welcome in the Indian village. There had been horse races between Indians and the Policemen, with much enthusiastic betting. Since no one had any money, the bets had to be paid off in kind rather than cash, and soon victorious Mounties were wrapping themselves in buffalo robes against the cold, while Indians became the proud possessors of treasures like watches, pocket knives and shaving mirrors.

Only one unfortunate incident had broken the general atmosphere of good will. Fred Denbow had decided to teach the Indians to play football. He'd set up goalposts, organised two opposing teams of Indians and Mounties, and the game had got off to an enthusiastic, if untidy, start.

Unfortunately Fred had tackled one opposing brave so hard that he'd crashed to the ground. The defeated warrior, unfamiliar with the rules of the game, had drawn his scalping-knife and chased Fred back to the Fort, ignoring the frantic whistle-blowing of the referee.

This morning's events were to be the climax of the visit. Macleod hoped it would interest and perhaps impress Chief Crowfoot to see the first trial to be held in the Fort.

Macleod took his place at the central table, flanked by two of his inspectors. In his role of the chief, and indeed only magistrate in the territory, he began the trial.

From the back of the court Crowfoot watched the strange proceedings with interest. The four whisky traders were brought in, chastened and subdued after a night in the Mounties' jail. Even they seemed impressed by the formality of the proceedings. Rob gave his evidence first, telling of his meeting with Two Bulls.

Then the huge warrior appeared, glaring round him suspiciously. With Jerry Potts interpreting, he told how the white men had traded him whisky for his goods. He identified the four men with a threatening shake of his fist. Then Rob resumed his testimony, telling how they'd tracked the two wagons. He told of his arrest of the traders, and of the whisky he had found in one of the wagons.

Macleod listened impassively, and when Rob sat down he turned to the four men. 'You have heard the evidence against you. Have you anything to say?'

The leader of the group, who had given his name as Joe Sanders, glared angrily at Macleod. 'See here, mister, we're all American citizens, and the goods in them wagons is American property. You let us go and give us our stuff back, or you're gonna be in mighty big trouble...' His voice tailed away under Macleod's hard stare.

Macleod said coldly, 'Is that all?' When Sanders didn't speak, he went on, 'Your nationality is irrelevant. You were on Canadian soil, and you have broken Canadian law. You will each be fined two hundred dollars. Your wagons and goods will be confiscated. The whisky will be destroyed.'

A gabble of angry protest went up from the four men. Macleod crashed his fist down on the table. 'Silence! I am treating you leniently, since this is the first time you have come before me. I advise you to go back across the border and spread the word amongst your associates. There will be no more whisky trading in the North-West.'

Sanders drawled, 'If this is what you call being lenient, mister, I'd hate to meet you when you're being tough!' The defendants were led out. Soon, broke and angry, they would be starting the long ride back to Fort Benton. Macleod was about to declare the court closed when Inspector Jarvis, who had been reading a note passed to him, leaned forward and whispered,

'Seems we've got another case for you, sir. You remember Deakin was out on patrol looking for whisky traders? Well, he didn't find any, but he's brought in some horse thieves.'

Macleod hesitated, then said, 'All right, bring them in. We may as well make a clean sweep.'

Three very angry Indians were ushered into the court by rifle carrying Mounties. At the sight of the tallest of them Rob leaped out of his seat. Ignoring court procedure he crossed to Macleod, who looked up angrily. 'What do you think you're doing, Mac-Gregor? Go back to your place.'

Unabashed, Rob whispered, 'You see that Indian there, sir, the tall one? His name's Red Crow.'

Macleod frowned, 'Well, what of it?'

'He happens to be Chief Crowfoot's son, sir. I just thought you ought to know.' And with that, Rob slipped back to his place.

Inspector Jarvis gave Macleod a puzzled look, wondering what was going on. 'Shall I continue, sir?'

For a moment Macleod said nothing, then he nodded abruptly. He gave a silent inward groan. What an unlucky thing to happen. Of all the Indians in the North-West, why did Deakin have to bring in Crowfoot's son?

Macleod listened gloomily to Deakin's evidence. He'd entered a Cree village, looking for information about the whisky traders, and had found a Cree war party about to set out after horse thieves. Deakin had persuaded the angry Indians to leave matters to the Police, and had set out on the trail of the stolen horses. Through a stroke of luck he had surprised them in camp, and had arrested the lot, bringing thieves, horses and complaining Crees back to the Fort.

When he'd heard all the evidence Macleod turned to Jerry Potts. 'Ask the prisoners if they've anything to say.'

Red Crow didn't need an interpreter. Indignantly, he burst out, 'Sure I steal Cree horses. Last year Crees steal horses from us, this year I steal from them.' He seemed to think this was an eminently fair arrangement.

Macleod looked round the crowded room while he collected his thoughts. He saw Chief Crowfoot watching him. There were only a few Indians in the courtroom, but there were hundreds of armed braves in the camp outside the Fort; if Crowfoot refused to accept the verdict...

Despite the difficult circumstances, Macleod had no choice. The Indians had seen that the law applied to white men. Now they must learn that it also applied to them. Gravely he said, 'I know it has long been the custom amongst Indians to steal horses from one another, that this is one of the ways in which your young men prove their skill and courage. But theft is theft, and the law forbids it. In the past such raids have led to bloodshed, and even to war. There must be no more of them. The stolen horses will be returned to the Crees. As compensation, Red Crow will give them two horses of his own. The prisoners may leave. The court is closed.'

The guards lowered their rifles and stepped back, and the confused Indians joined the crowd straggling out of the room. Rob saw Red Crow pause by his father, and they spoke quickly together in the Blackfoot tongue.

Macleod came out from behind his table and walked up to Crowfoot, who stood waiting, fanning himself, a fan made from an eagle's wing. For a moment the two men confronted each other. Then Crowfoot said solemnly, 'I see that your justice is indeed the same for all. If you punish the whisky trader, shall you not also rebuke the stealer of horses?'

Commissioner and Chief left the courtroom side by side, chatting amiably. Quite a friendship had sprung up between them, and clearly this incident had done nothing to spoil it. Rob pushed his way out to the compound where a crestfallen Red Crow was being mocked by his friends. Red Crow said, 'Hah, Mas-gwa-ah-sid! When I save you from Sioux, I don't think you send red coats to arrest me!'

Rob shook his Indian friend by the hand. 'Well, you got off pretty lightly. I couldn't believe it when they brought you in.'

Red Crow said, 'Chief forbid horse-stealing raids. I tell him I go hunt buffalo. How you think I feel, coming in talk-place see father there?'

Red Crow was obviously far more worried about his father's reaction than that of the Police. 'Tell me,' asked Rob, 'what did he say to you in court?'

Red Crow looked shamefaced. 'Say I big fool to steal horse from Cree, and *plenty* big fool to get caught by Mounties!'

Next day the Indians left the Fort. Crowfoot promised to return soon, bringing more chiefs for a conference. The friendship between Commissioner and Indian Chief was based on mutual respect. Macleod felt Crowfoot's visit had done much to establish friendly relations with the Indians. Amongst many other matters, they had discussed the Cypress Hills massacre. Macleod promised Crowfoot that he would extradite the guilty men from America, and have them tried for their crimes.

Once the Indians were gone, life at Fort Macleod returned to its normal routine. Their visit and the accompanying festivities, not least the trial of the whisky traders, had provided entertainment and distraction. Now that the everyday monotony of life returned, the grumbles and complaints of the men came flooding back.

Rob discussed the situation with his friends as they sat over their afternoon meal of bread and tea. The pieces of bread were getting smaller these days, and the tea weaker. Even the usually cheerful Fred was down-hearted. 'Dash it all,' he spluttered, 'I hate a whiner, Rob, you know that. But this isn't just the usual grumbling. The men have got genuine complaints, and they're nearing the end of their patience.'

Henri agreed. 'Some of the biggest grumblers are spending a lot of time together.' He indicated a corner table, where a few constables formed a separate group, their heads together over their tea. Rob took a quick look at them. 'Evans, Cooper, LeBrun, Henson ... why are they so thick all of a sudden?'

Henri shrugged. 'Perhaps they are planning something.'

Rob and Fred looked at each other, as they took in the implications of Henri's remark.

Rob said slowly, 'You really think so?'

'There has been much talking in corners, many conversations that end when someone comes near.'

'Misery loves company,' said Fred. 'Probably just having a good old buck.' 'A buck' was Mountie slang for any kind of grumble or complaint.

Henri wasn't convinced. 'Unless something is done very soon, my friends, there is going to be a very big buck—the biggest this Force has ever seen.'

Henri was proved right the very next morning. When reveille sounded everyone rose as usual, encouraged by the shouts and jibes from Sergeant Reilly. But when bugle call rang for morning stables, a group of men, centred round Constable Evans, made no attempt to move. Henri looked at his two friends. 'You see?' he said simply.

'We'd better find out what's going on,' said Rob. The three friends wandered over to Evans's bed. Rob gave him a friendly nod. 'You lot are taking it pretty easy. You'll be late for stables.'

'Oh no we won't, boyo, 'cause we're not going. We're not answering another bugle call till something's done about our complaints.' He raised his voice, looking round the large barrack room. 'Any of you with the guts to stand up for themselves will stay here with us.'

'Have some sense, man. This is plain stupid.'

'Oh, we didn't expect any help from you, MacGregor. Everyone knows you're the Commissioner's little pet.'

Rob grabbed the lanky policeman, shook him till his teeth rattled and threw him back on his bed. 'I'm nobody's little pet,' he growled. 'I'm not saying you haven't got grievances. But this isn't the way to settle them.'

When his breath came back, Evans shouted, 'Oh no? Then what is?'

'Form a delegation. Make an official request to see Macleod. I'll go myself if you like.' Rob too raised his voice. 'If we act like grown-ups there's a chance to get something done. We'll get nowhere sulking like children.'

A babble of argument and discussion filled the barrack room. Evans renewed his urge to disobey orders, but it was clear that the majority of the men sided with Rob. He might have won them over altogether, if Sergeant Reilly hadn't stormed into the barrack room and started screaming orders to get on parade at once—or else!

The men were in no mood to be bullied. Immediately the feeling in the room swung back towards Evans, who took full advantage of his chance. 'Or else what?' he shouted triumphantly. 'We're not the army, we're a civil force. You know the worst he can do to us? Fine us! Fine us when we haven't a cent to our names!'

That clinched it. There was a yell of mocking laughter.

Sergeant Reilly turned scarlet with rage. 'Every man in this room is under arrest,' he roared. 'Stay here the lot of you!'

'Don't worry,' said Evans. 'That's just what we're going to do!'

Reilly marched out. Rob turned dismally to Fred and Henri. 'That's done it! They were starting to see some sense, but Reilly's sent them the other way. They're bound to stick up for Evans now.'

It certainly looked as if Evans had won. The men crowded round him, pouring out their grievances, and Evans made lavish promises that everything would be put right. He sat on his bed surrounded by an admiring crowd. 'When I see Macleod,' he yelled, 'I shall tell him something, never fear!'

'Tell him what, Constable Evans?' asked a deep voice. A sudden appalled silence filled the room. Commissioner Macleod stood at the entrance, his burly frame filling the doorway. He strolled coolly into the room full of angry and excited men. When Sergeant Reilly had come to him, spluttering demands for an armed party to arrest the entire barrack room, Macleod pointed out that if they arrested over fifty men they'd have nowhere to put them anyway. Refusing any escort he'd decided to deal with the matter in person.

Evans was in too deep to back down now, and gathering his nerve he began stammering out a list of the men's many grievances. Macleod listened quietly, until Evans had finished. Suddenly he turned to Rob and his friends, who had been standing slightly apart from the others. 'What about you, Constable MacGregor? Where do you stand in all this?'

Rob's heart sank as he heard the Commissioner single him out. He really was in the hot seat now. He felt no desire to ally himself with Evans. At the same time, he didn't want to be branded before the men as teacher's pet, always currying favour with the Commissioner. Rob decided that since he was caught in the middle anyway, he might as well be honest. 'I think Evans is right, sir,' he said boldly. A murmur of surprise went up, and Evans shot him a look of pure astonishment. 'Mind you, I don't agree with this business of disobeying orders. That's plain daft, and I was just now saying so. As for the conditions—well, we knew it'd be tough when we joined, and they'll get better in time. But the fact we've had no pay for over six months—well, I think that's a fair disgrace!' Feeling sure he'd talked away his Mounted Police career, Rob folded his arms and glared defiantly at Macleod. He hadn't wanted the position of spokesman, but since it had been thrust upon him, he decided to make the best of it. There were mutters of agreement from the men. Most of them found Rob a far more acceptable leader than Evans.

Every eye in the room was fixed upon Macleod, wondering how he would react to Rob's defiant speech. The Commissioner was silent for a moment, then suddenly boomed, 'I absolutely agree with you, Constable MacGregor. It *is* a disgrace. I've sent message after message to Ottowa saying so.' Astonished to find the Commissioner on their side, the men didn't know where they were. 'Late last night,' Macleod continued, 'I received an answer. The Government has arranged for a bank in Helena, Montana, to advance all necessary funds. I am setting off for Helena tomorrow. You will all be paid as soon as I return.' His last few words were drowned by excited cheering. Macleod raised his voice above the hubbub. 'I shall need two constables to accompany me. You'd better be one of them, MacGregor. And the other ... yes, I think you, Evans.' Evans looked far from delighted with the honour.

Macleod produced his pocket watch and glanced at it. 'Today's records will show that stable call was postponed—for administrative reasons.' He glanced meaningfully around the room. 'That is *all* they will show. Prepare to get moving, gentlemen, the bugle will sound in a few minutes. You'll have to work extra hard to make up lost time.' As suddenly as he had arrived, Macleod was gone.

Once more there was a hum of excited comment. Men crowded round Rob, slapping him on the back and congratulating him on the way he'd spoken up. Vastly embarrassed, Rob shook them off. He went across to Evans who was sitting forgotten on his bed. '*You* don't seem very happy. You're getting what you wanted, aren't you?'

'I didn't want a trip to Montana,' said Evans gloomily. 'You realise where Helena is, boyo? Three hundred miles across the Badlands. And it's still winter! We'll be lucky to get there alive. And as for getting back ...'

Rob slapped him on the back. 'Serves you right, man. That's what you get for making speeches.'

Stable call rang out for the second time that morning, and the men began hurrying from the room. The 'big buck' was over.

5

Across the Badlands

Commissioner Macleod shrugged himself into the huge fur coat and pulled the hat down on to his head. With his bushy black beard jutting out from the furs, he looked like a bad-tempered grizzly bear. 'Ready, Jerry?'

The little scout sighed. 'Sure, me *ready . . .*'

'But not exactly willing, eh?'

'Government damn fools. They don't know country here. I do. Nobody cross Badlands in winter. Better you wait till spring.'

'I can't,' said Macleod simply. 'The men have waited long enough; I must get that pay as soon as possible. You can get us through, Jerry.'

Jerry shrugged. 'Maybe. All the same, bad time to travel. Blackfoot never go long journey in winter. Bad medicine.'

'That doesn't worry you, does it? You're not an Indian.'

'Half-Indian. That half worry plenty.'

'Well, just you listen to the Scottish half. We're going to Montana!'

Macleod strode from the room, and Jerry followed. Outside in the compound, Rob and Evans were waiting, both wearing winter kit. Each was mounted and ready, and each led a loaded pack horse.

Macleod looked at them approvingly. 'You've

checked the supplies, Constable MacGregor?'

'Yes, sir. Blankets, buffalo robes, boiled bacon and hard-tack and tea for us, oats for the horses.'

Macleod took the reins of his big black stallion from a waiting constable and swung into the saddle. The little cavalcade set off on its long and dangerous journey.

They made good time on their first day. The weather stayed clear, and Rob felt exhilarated to be on the move again. Even the pessimistic Evans began to look a little more cheerful. That night they camped in the ruins of Fort Whoop-Up, the whisky traders' fort that Rob had helped to find and close down. To their surprise, the Fort was partially repaired and in use again. A grey-haired old man with a game leg hobbled to open the gate for them. 'Name's Dave,' he said, 'Dave Akers.' Macleod asked what he was doing there. Akers explained that after the Fort had been partially burned down, the I.G. Baker company in Fort Benton had taken it over for use as a trading post. The old man looked anxiously at them. 'Just the ordinary trade goods, no whisky here, I promise you. Whisky traders keep well away since you boys came.'

Rob looked round. The Fort had been strongly built, and quite a few of the main buildings had survived the fire. It was strange to think that this was the notorious Fort Whoop-Up, where hundreds of armed outlaws had defied the law. Now it was just a simple trading post. It was a change for the better, thought Rob. He was glad he'd been able to help to bring it about. And at least the partial restoration of the Fort meant they could spend the night under cover.

Old Dave, anxious to keep in well with the Mounties, insisted on cooking them an excellent supper. From the trade goods on his shelves he prepared a thick and nourishing stew of canned meat, dried peas and potatoes. An even greater luxury was the dessert—canned peaches eaten frontier-style, straight from the tin. Rob was feeling well-fed and contented as he strolled into the compound after supper. Jerry Potts stood looking up at the brilliant sunset with an expression of deepest gloom. 'Very bad,' was all he would say. 'Big snow soon.'

In the days that followed, it seemed Jerry was no weather prophet, for the weather continued good, very cold but dry and clear. In fact they were nearing the end of the journey before Jerry's words came true. One morning after breakfast, Rob was checking the load of his pack-pony, when a flake of snow landed on the end of his nose. He looked up at the winter sky. More and more flakes were falling, softly, silently. It continued snowing all day, and soon a wind sprang up, driving the snow into their faces. It was dry and hard, and seemed to cut like a million tiny knives. The wind grew stronger. They had to dismount and plod forward on foot, leading the horses. Hour after hour they struggled on in the face of what was now a howling blizzard. The wind was up to fifty miles an hour, and the temperature well below zero.

Macleod plodded to Jerry's side and bent down to shout over the noise of the wind. 'We can't keep this up much longer, Jerry.' His voice was calm, just stating the facts. Men and horses were reaching the limits of their endurance.

'We stop here, we die,' yelled Jerry, waving around at the flat, snow-driven plains. 'Got to reach Milk River. Maybe find shelter.' They plodded forward, Rob and Evans behind them. Rob kept his head down, trying to keep the driving snow out of his eyes. All he could see was the snowy ground and the moving hooves of the horse in front. Long hours later, they reached Milk River. Jerry took them to a deep ravine, where sloping sides gave shelter from the worst of the blizzard. He pointed to a snowbank and yelled, 'Dig!'

They dug. With their knives they hacked out an enormous cave in the snowy bank, Macleod working harder than any of them. When it was finished the cave was big enough for all, men *and* horses, to huddle inside, away from the howling winds.

Jerry Potts said, 'O.K!' He set off into the storm.

Macleod shouted, 'Jerry, where are you going?'

'Find wood for fire.'

Rob was bone weary but he couldn't let Jerry go alone.

Evans was slumped on the ground, no use to anyone. With a glance at Macleod, Rob said, 'Hold on, Jerry, I'll give you a hand.' As they stumbled out into the storm, Rob yelled, 'What exactly are we looking for?'

'Old wagon, smashed up. I remember it from last spring.'

They searched for quite a while without finding the wagon. Visibility was down to a few feet in the driving snow, and Rob was ready to give up when he tripped on something hard beneath the snow and fell flat on his face. He groped with mittened hands and found the round shape of a wagon wheel. He gave an exultant yell. 'Here it is, Jerry.'

They dug the snow clear of the broken wagon, kicked boards and planks from the sides and dragged them into the cave. After several journeys they had enough wood in the cave to keep a fire going.

Macleod and Evans pitched camp, and soon they were sitting round a blaze munching hard biscuits and half-cooked bacon, and drinking hot tea.

Macleod looked round at his shivering command and ordered, 'Don't sit there moping, let's have a song!' And sing they did. Scottish folk ballads, old pioneer songs, mournful Welsh ballads from Evans, and strange Indian chants from Jerry Potts.

They stayed in the snow-cave all night, all the following day, and all the next night. Things weren't too bad the first night. They collapsed into an exhausted sleep round the fire. The next day dragged by slowly, with the temperature well below zero. By now the wood from the broken wagon was exhausted, and a further search by Rob and Jerry failed to reveal any more. They huddled inside their furs, occasionally stamping up and down to keep the blood circulating. It was on the second night that things got really bad. Rob was awakened from an uneasy sleep by the sound of pounding feet. The horses were stamping about, whickering nervously.

He peered out into the darkness. Enormous shapes were moving about outside the cave. Rob struggled to his feet and went to his horse, holding it by the halter-rope and trying to calm it. Dimly he saw Jerry Potts nearby. 'What's happening?'

'Buffalo! Come down to river for shelter. Big herd all round us.'

Rob managed a weary grin. 'This is a fine big cave, but I don't think we've room for a herd of buffalo as well. They'll have to take their chances outside.'

Macleod and Evans joined them and they spent the rest of the night taking turns to hold the horses, soothing them and preventing them from wandering off. When daylight came they found themselves on the edge of a huge herd, crowded into the river valley for shelter.

Jerry looked at the blizzard which showed no signs of dying down. 'We go on. Too cold to stop more.'

Huddled in his blankets, Evans moaned, 'I can't go on. I can't move.'

Jerry looked at him. 'You stay, you die.' He led his horse out of the cave. One by one the others followed, Evans trailing in the rear.

Once more the nightmare journey through the storm began. Rob plodded on steadily, his mind and body too numb to think. After a while he wondered how Evans was doing and turned to look. To his horror the man was nowhere in sight. Rob managed to alert Jerry and Macleod with a croaking shout. Wearily, every step a tremendous effort, they went back to look for him. They found him at last, sitting in the snow clutching the reins of his horse. Rob tried to lift him to his feet. 'Come on, man, we've got to keep moving or we'll die.'

Evans made no attempt to stir. He gazed up at Rob, his face rimmed with snow. 'Rob, is that you? You'll have to leave me. I can't go on—I can't see...'

Jerry Potts looked down into the staring eyes. 'Snowblind,' he said.

Somehow they managed to lift Evans on to his horse, tying him on with rope from the saddle-bags. Macleod led Evans's horse as well as his own. Jerry and Rob were already leading a horse and a pack pony. Each man dragging two horses behind him, they set off into the storm.

The end when it came was very sudden. They heard the jingle of harness and shouted orders. Suddenly they were surrounded by mounted men. A cloaked figure lent from his saddle thrusting a carbine at them. 'Hold it right there, gents.' Over his shoulder he yelled, 'I got 'em, Lootenant. Whisky peddlers for sure. Who else'd be out in this kind of storm?'

Macleod straightened up. Thrusting out his black beard he roared at the astonished sergeant, 'I am not a whisky trader, I am Commissioner Macleod of the North-West Mounted Police.'

A very young Lieutenant of U.S. Cavalry rode up, 'What's going on here, Sergeant?'

The Sergeant scratched his chin. 'Well, he looks like a whisky trader, sir. But he sure don't sound like one.'

Once they'd convinced the cavalry patrol of their identity the worst was over. The lieutenant took them into Fort Shaw, where Evans was left to recover from his snow blindness. The men of the U.S. Cavalry plied them with food and drink, unable to believe they'd actually made it across the Badlands.

Next day, after a long and enjoyable sleep, Commissioner Macleod, Jerry Potts and Constable Rob MacGregor set off for Helena, Montana. They didn't realise it, but their real troubles were only just beginning.

6

'You want 'em, you find 'em!'

Boom time had come to the small frontier town of Helena, Montana. Gold had been discovered near by, and the muddy streets were thronged with prospectors, miners, cowboys, trappers, soldiers—all the colourful population of a western town.

Wrapped in their furs, Macleod, Rob and Jerry attracted no particular notice as they rode through the crowded streets.

They found a quiet back street hotel, turned their horses over to the livery stable and set out to find the bank. Glancing round as they shouldered their way through the jostling crowd, Rob thought he'd never seen such a tough-looking crowd in his life. One thing struck him immediately. In Canada men went armed only if there was specific need, such as a journey through dangerous country. But on the American side of the border, even in a biggish town like Helena, everyone seemed to carry a gun automatically.

The President of the Bank was a big, portly man, gold watch-chain stretched tight over the swelling curve of his fancy waistcoat. He welcomed them politely in his luxurious oak-panelled office, but was obviously surprised to see them.

'Sure your credit's good, Commissioner, the draft

arrived a while ago. Take us till tomorrow to have the money ready though. We weren't expecting to see you till spring. You really crossed the Badlands this time of year?'

'We would scarcely be here if we had not, sir,' said Macleod briskly. 'I should be glad if you would have the money made up. Coin and small bills, please, it is to be distributed amongst a large number of men. I'll call for it in the morning.'

'Be glad to oblige, sir. Forgive me for asking, but do you plan to take this money back yourselves? Just the three of you?'

'Of course.'

'Then you'd better hire an escort. Thirty thousand dollars is a mighty big sum. There are plenty of men in Helena who'd shoot you for less than that.'

Macleod said, 'I can think of no better way to attract their attention than by surrounding the money with a large number of guards. Just make the money up, sir, and I'll collect it tomorrow. Now, if you'll excuse me, I have other business to attend to.'

As Macleod led them out of the bank, Rob and Jerry exchanged wondering glances. This was the first they'd heard of a second reason for coming to Helena. Macleod led them down the main street to a sturdy square building that stood some way from the others. The windows were barred and a sign hanging over the door read, 'Sheriff's Office and Jail'. Macleod pushed open the door and they followed him inside.

They found themselves in a small square room furnished with a massive roll-topped desk and a few battered chairs. There was a gun-rack on one wall, and other walls were decorated with a variety of 'Wanted' posters, many faded and yellowing. An iron grille barred a corridor that obviously led to the jail section, and a huge pot-bellied stove glowed red in the centre of the room. Behind the big desk sat a tall thin man with a long drooping moustache. He wore a black suit, a broad-brimmed black hat, two Colt ·45 revolvers and a silver star. He looked up as they crowded into his office. 'Come right in, gents, make yourselves at home.'

Macleod identified himself and produced his credentials. The Sheriff's eyes widened as he saw the scarlet tunic beneath the furs. 'You're a long way from home, Commissioner. What can I do for you?'

Calmly Macleod said, 'You can help me to find and arrest the men responsible for the Cypress Hills massacre.

The Sheriff looked baffled. 'The what?'

'Two years ago a party of American trappers shot down a number of Indians in the Cypress Hills. At that time there was no law-enforcement agency to deal with them. Now there is. Those men committed murder on Canadian soil, Sheriff, and I want them.'

The Sheriff tugged thoughtfully at the ends of his long moustache. 'Well, sure you do, Commissioner, and I can't say I blame you. Thing is, it's kinda complicated. Do you know who they are?'

'Not yet. My information is that these men are living in or near Fort Benton. It shouldn't be too difficult to trace them.'

'Don't be too sure. They could have changed their names or moved on by now. Even if you do find them, they're American citizens, and they're back on American soil. They'll have to be extradited. That means a hearing, here in Helena. You'll have to produce witnesses, show just cause for extradition.'

'Then that's what we'll do. There must be plenty of people who know who they are and what they've done.'

The Sheriff sighed. This big, bearded Commissioner didn't seem willing to take no for an answer. 'Maybe there are. But will they testify against them in court? You know the law, Commissioner, it ain't knowing it's proving.' The Sheriff looked a little shamefaced as he went on, 'You see, we look at things kinda different this side of the border. We been fighting Indians so long, it's hard to think of killing 'em as a crime.'

'Does that apply to the killing of women and children too?'

'I'm not saying it's right, Commissioner. I'm just telling you the way it is.'

Macleod gave an impatient snort. Wearily the Sheriff said, 'Exactly what do you want me to do?'

'I want you to send an official request to the Sheriff in Fort Benton to find and arrest these men and send them here for an extradition hearing.'

The Sheriff stood up and stretched. 'Sure I can do that. If you want to put paid for good to your chances of getting them.'

He wandered across to the jail area and glanced through. In one of the cells, a solitary drunk was sleeping it off. The Sheriff turned back to Macleod.

'Over here a Sheriff is *elected*, you see. If the Sheriff in Fort Benton picks up those men for you, he'll be running mighty short of votes come next election-time. Now I know old Luke Hancock and he's mighty fond of his job. Chances are, word would somehow reach those men, and they'd just kinda take off for the hills. You want 'em, you find 'em yourself, that's my advice.'

Macleod had always been determined to bring the Cypress Hills murderers to justice. The job of getting the Force out to the North-West and firmly established there had meant that the business had been postponed. Now it looked as if he'd left things too late. What had seemed a clear-cut case was turning into a complicated political mess of the kind he hated most. 'Well, Sheriff, is there anything you *can* do to help us?'

'I'll go to the courts and start the arrangements for an extradition hearing. That's the best I can do. You staying in Helena a while?'

Macleod shook his head. 'I'm leaving tomorrow, as soon as I've collected my money.' He explained about the payroll, refusing the Sheriff's offer of a posse of deputies to guard it.

The Sheriff opened the door. 'You bring me those men, Commissioner, and I'll see they're brought to trial. Good luck!' It was clear that he didn't expect to see them again.

That night, Macleod, Jerry and Rob held a conference over dinner in their little hotel. Macleod looked around his tiny command, one constable and one scout, and spoke as if he were addressing an entire troop. 'It seems to me that we have three problems, gentlemen. We have to find and identify these men. We have to provide witnesses against them. Finally we must secure their arrest before they can escape. And the last problem is the biggest. We've no jurisdiction outside of Canada, and it seems we'll get little help from the law in Fort Benton.'

'What will you do, sir?' asked Rob. It was clear from Macleod's expression that he'd already found an answer.

'I shall use the United States Army. There's a post in Fort Benton, and if I make an official request, I'm sure they'll co-operate. Soldiers, at least, aren't elected.' Macleod looked quizzically at Rob. 'Well, I've solved one of our problems. If you're willing, I think you could solve another—finding and identifying these men.'

'You want me to work undercover again, sir?'

'I'm afraid it's the only way. Anyone who knows the whereabouts of these people will only talk in front of someone of their own kind.'

Rob was far from overjoyed at the thought of taking off his uniform and pretending to be some kind of border ruffian. Nevertheless he knew Macleod was right. 'I'll do the best I can, sir.'

'Then that only leaves one problem. Witnesses.'

Jerry Potts said, 'Abe Farwell.'

The other two looked at him in astonishment. They were so used to Jerry's long periods of silence that it was always something of a shock when he actually spoke. As always, Jerry didn't waste words. 'Farwell ran a trading post. See massacre, can't stop it.

76

Run away and hide afterwards.'

Macleod leaned forward eagerly, 'Where did he go?'

'Farwell have Blackfoot wife, I think he with her, back to her people, hide in village.'

'Can you find him?'

'I find.'

As the three of them spent the rest of the evening working out their plans, an old drunk was being released from the Helena jail. He weaved his way to a saloon in the toughest part of town, cadged a drink from a sympathetic friend, and began telling a muddled story of soldiers in scarlet coats who had come to pick up vast sums of money and arrest all the Cypress Hills killers in Fort Benton. The stories got wilder with every drink, and no one really paid very much attention. Except for one man sitting by himself in a corner of the saloon. A very tall, very thin man, with a bony, skull-like face, and long, greasy yellow hair. He went up to the bar, bought a bottle of whisky, grabbed the old drunk and shoved him down at a quiet corner table. He tapped the full bottle. 'This is for you, old man—if you tell me everything you heard in that jail.' The old man reached out a trembling hand. He snatched it back as the blade of a Bowie knife rapped him painfully across the knuckles. 'I want *just* what you heard, and no more,' said the stranger coldly. He twisted the knife so that the lamplight flickered on the blade.

The old man made a desperate attempt to gather his wandering wits. 'Sure, I'll tell you, mister, and every word the gospel truth.' Thirsting for the whisky, terrified of the shining knife-blade, he began to talk.

Next morning Rob and Jerry bought supplies for the journey back, and a civilian outfit for Rob. Macleod had already collected the money, carrying it back through the streets in a sack over his shoulder, as casually as if it had been a sack of oats. The plan was that Rob should ride with them to Fort Shaw, where they would pick up Constable Evans, who should now be over his snow-blindness. Then Rob, in civilian disguise, would begin making his way to Fort Benton, to start the search for the wanted men, while the others took the money back to Fort Macleod. Once that was done, Jerry would ride into Blackfoot country to look for Abe Farwell, the only known witness to the crime.

They all met in the stables behind the hotel, and began saddling and loading their horses. Without looking up from his task, Jerry said quietly, 'Somebody watching us.' Taking their cue from Jerry the others continued working quietly.

'You're sure, Jerry?' said Rob.

'Watching hotel in morning. Three, four men. Follow me an' Rob to store, follow Commissioner to bank and back.'

Macleod remembered how casually he'd carried the money. 'You might have warned me, Jerry.'

'No need. They don't try anything in town. Follow us, attack in Badlands.'

Obviously Jerry had some kind of plan. 'What do

you want us to do now?' asked the Commissioner.

'You pay me off here, like hired guide. Make big fuss. Then you leave town. They follow you, I follow them.'

They played out the little comedy as Jerry suggested. When the loading was finished, Macleod produced money and gave some to Jerry. Jerry looked at it in indignation and demanded more. Macleod refused loudly and indignantly. When Jerry tried to snatch the money Rob gave him a shove that sent him reeling into the mud. Jerry backed away down the street shouting threats and curses. Macleod and Rob saddled up and began riding away, Rob leading the pack ponies.

As they jogged along the trail that led to the edge of town, Rob said, 'I wonder how Jerry's getting on, sir?'

Macleod grunted. 'I'd be a lot happier if I knew. He's got all the initiative, and we're the sitting ducks.' It was hard to ride along looking relaxed and carefree, knowing that armed killers were planning an attack. Rob glanced uneasily at Macleod's saddle-bow where the sack of money was fastened. It looked as if their plan to sneak the money out of town unnoticed had already failed. Rob would have been a lot happier with an armed escort beside them.

Nothing happened for quite a long time. The buildings gradually thinned out, and soon they were away from town altogether. They rode on, the trail taking them into hilly, broken country. At last Macleod pointed ahead to where the trail passed through an outcrop of ragged rocks. 'That looks a likely place.

Plenty of cover, somewhere to hide the bodies.' Rob shivered. How could Macleod be so calm, when the 'bodies' he referred to might be their own.

'What do we do, sir?'

'Trust Jerry. He's never let us down yet. Still, just in case there is a hitch...' Macleod unbuttoned the flap of the holster and drew his Adams revolver, keeping it ready in his hand but hidden under his furs. Rob did the same, and the two rode slowly forward.

As they passed between the big clumps of boulders, Rob began to wonder if Macleod was right. Would the ambush take place here? Suddenly, at a point where the trail bent sharply and disappeared behind some rocks, they heard a rider coming towards them. Rob took a tighter grip on his revolver, and glanced at Macleod, who frowned warningly. The unseen rider was approaching slowly with no attempt at concealment. They didn't want to shoot some innocent traveller. The hoofbeats drew nearer and nearer, and a rider appeared round the rocks. Rob tensed. The man was short and plump, with a round, cheerful face. He appeared to be unarmed, and raised his hand in a peaceful salute. 'Hi there, gents. Would you be those policemen fellers from Canada?'

Macleod said grimly, 'We would.'

'Carrying that nice fat payroll for all them hard-up Mounties?' There was a mocking note in the voice now.

'I don't think that concerns you.'

'Well, I can tell you something that concerns *you*, Mister Policeman, I got men covering you with rifles from both sides of the road.'

Rob and Macleod glanced up. High in the rocks riflemen had appeared, two on the right side of the trail, one to the left. Scarves were pulled up to hide their faces. Macleod looked back at the rider on the trail. 'What do you want?'

'First you hand over that payroll nice and peaceful. Then you get down from your horses and have a little chat with me and my boys. You fellers have got to be taught to mind your own affairs. The lesson's gonna be expensive. Expensive and painful.'

Rob looked at Macleod. It was easy to guess what the fat little thug had in mind. They were to be robbed and beaten-up, sent back to Canada with nothing but bruises to show for their journey. Rob glanced quickly at Macleod, wondering what he would do. Not surrender tamely, that was for sure. It was true the riflemen had them covered. But they didn't know that both Macleod and Rob already had revolvers in their hands. If the killers weren't expecting sudden resistance, they might stand a chance. And there was still Jerry Potts...

Macleod spurred his horse forward. 'Get out of my way, or you'll be sorry.'

The round-faced man yelled, 'O.K., let 'em have it.' At the same time he grabbed for a hidden revolver.

Everything happened very fast. Macleod rode his big stallion straight into the outlaw's pony, sending the lighter horse staggering back, and spoiling the man's aim. Rob pulled out his revolver and blazed away at the two riflemen high on his right. He saw the fat man recover his balance first, and take point-blank aim at Macleod, who was struggling to control his horse. A shot rang out—and the fat man tumbled to the ground. But whose shot? Rob looked up and saw the solitary rifleman to his left firing not at them, but at his two fellows on the other side of the trail. One of them yelped and rolled over, clutching at his shoulder. The other turned and ran for it, his long-legged form leaping over the rocks like a mountain goat, yellow hair streaming out behind him. He disappeared from view behind the rocks, and a moment later they heard the sound of hoof beats charging into the distance. The remaining rifleman picked his way down the rocks towards them. Macleod and Rob waited with drawn revolvers. The man pulled the scarf from his face and yelled, 'Hey, don't shoot. It's me ... Jerry!'

When their enthusiastic welcome was over, Jerry explained. The playacting at the hotel had worked even better than hoped. As soon as Rob and Macleod rode off, three men had approached him, full of sympathy, and offering him a drink. In a nearby saloon, Jerry had played the part of the disgruntled guide, dissatisfied with his fee. The leader of the three men, the one with long yellow hair, had offered him the chance of revenge. They would all select a suitable spot and lay on an ambush. Several drinks later, Jerry had allowed himself to be persuaded. Soon he had found himself riding to attack Rob and Macleod. They'd hidden their horses near the trail and waited.

Macleod looked down at the body of the fat man. 'If you hadn't been so quick to shoot, Jerry, this one might have told us something.'

Jerry looked hurt. 'I don't kill him, he kill you,' he

pointed out reproachfully. 'Anyway, still got one left.' Jerry climbed back up into the rocks and soon reappeared, pushing a moaning, complaining man before them. The wounded outlaw was a typical bar-room thug, burly and unshaven.

Macleod questioned him sternly, but learned little. He and his tubby friend had been recruited the night before by the man with long hair. 'Said it was a chance at some easy money,' muttered the man, wincing as Jerry bandaged his wound. 'Now just look at me.'

Macleod was unsympathetic. 'Easy money comes hard sometimes.' He turned to Rob and Jerry. 'One dead, one wounded, one escaped. Not a perfect score, but it could be worse.' Rob said nothing. Reaction to the sudden flurry of shooting had left him weak and trembling, and he could only stare in horror at the fat outlaw's body, laying like an old sack on the muddy trail. Macleod followed his gaze. 'I know how you feel, boy. But remember this. If things had gone *his* way, that would have been you and me down there. Let's be on our way.'

7

The Claim Jumpers

It wasn't much of a mine. Just a cave hacked out of the hillside with a stream near by to wash out the ore. But it was the first gold-mine Rob had ever seen, and he looked at it in fascination. It was hard to realise that this untidy rock-pile could make anyone rich.

As he looked, three men came out of the cave, arguing furiously. One was a big, white-haired, whiskery old man, his once-powerful shoulders bowed and stooped with age. The others were younger, mining camp toughs of the sort Rob had seen in Helena. The old man made a final dismissive gesture and turned to go back into the cave. At this, one of the toughs reached under his coat and pulled out a cudgel. Instinctively Rob yelled out, 'Hold it!'

The tough with the cudgel froze, the weapon still in mid-air. The old miner turned, saw what had so nearly happened and knocked the tough to the ground with a tremendous blow of one of his big, gnarled fists. The second thug reached inside his ragged coat and Rob saw the flash of a knife-blade. He pulled his Colt from the waistband of his trousers, and fired a shot in the air. 'Just drop that knife,' he ordered. Sullenly the man obeyed. Rob walked his horse closer, and jumped down. By now the first tough was climbing dazedly to his feet. Rob was careful to keep both men covered with his revolver. 'All-right,' he said, 'get on your way.'

The old miner grabbed the first thug, spun him round and delivered a tremendous kick that sent the man rolling down the hillside to land in the stream below. 'You heard him—git!' he roared. The second thug ran after the first, and the two disappeared from sight.

Rob looked at the old man. 'Who were they?'

'Just a couple of claim-jumpers. Offering me a partnership.' The old man spat. 'I know the sort of partnership they had in mind—I do the work and they take the money.' He looked up at Rob, blue eyes sparkling brightly above his tangle of white beard. 'I'm obliged to you, boy.' He glanced up at the sky. 'Near enough time to eat. Care to join me? Only beans, bacon and coffee, but you're welcome.'

They ate sitting outside the cave. When the meal was over, Rob thanked the old miner and started to go on his way. The old man said, 'Just you wait a bit, young feller, I got a proposition for you. How'd you like to stay on here and help me out?'

Rob shook his head. 'Sorry, I've got to be moving on.'

The old miner held up his hand, 'I don't say she's a rich lode, but there's gold for both of us if we work at it. You won't do no better by yourself. The good claims are already gone by now. Think about it.'

Rob thought about it. After the attempted ambush, he'd ridden on with Macleod and Jerry. They'd taken the wounded outlaw (and the dead one) to Fort Shaw and handed them over to the Army. Then Macleod, Jerry and the now recovered Constable Evans had set off on the return journey to Canada, with a cavalry escort to see them as far as the border. Rob had changed into the outfit bought for him in Helena, rough second-hand clothing suitable for the young drifter he was to become. The outfit included the battered but still serviceable Colt that had just come in so handy. Riding a scrubby-looking cow pony (Brownie had been sent back to Fort Macleod) he had set off for Helena to begin his investigations. He planned to pick up what information he could in Helena, and then move on to Fort Benton, crossing back into Canada when his mission was completed. Jerry meanwhile would be searching the Blackfoot villages for the missing Abe Farwell and his Indian wife.

As he drunk the sweet black coffee and put down the battered tin cup, Rob was having second thoughts about the old miner's offer. A few days mining would give him a useful and genuine background. What better explanation for his presence in Helena? Rob knew he would be dealing with dangerous and suspicious men. The more convincing his cover story, the longer he was likely to live. He nodded to the old man. 'Thing is, I've got business to see to, so I couldn't stay long. But I'll give you a hand for a day or so, if that's any use.'

The old man stuck out a big hand. 'Shake on her. Name's Daniels. You can call me Pop.'

Rob took the big calloused hand and shook it. 'My name's Rob.' The old man made no attempt to ask Rob's surname, or anything about his business. In the west it was extremely impolite, and sometimes downright dangerous, to pry into the affairs of others.

Rob spent the best part of a week working with Pop Daniels in his little mine. It was a primitive enough affair. They hacked the ore out of the hillside with pick-axes, crushed it with sledge hammers, and dragged it down to the stream to sieve out the gold. It was hard, back-breaking work, and judging by the small amounts of gold that Pop finally sieved from the piles of rock, the rewards were modest at best. But Pop had been a miner all his life, making and spending several fortunes like others of his kind. As they sat round their campfire at night, he told Rob stories of fortunes won and lost in the great gold-rush of forty-nine.

At the end of the week Rob said goodbye to Pop Daniels with real regret. He'd grown very fond of the old man, and it was genuinely hard to resist his appeals to stay on. He even offered Rob a partnership. At last, realising Rob was determined, the old man carefully shook gold-dust into a wash-leather bag, Rob's share of their week's earnings, and sent him on his way. By now Rob had the calloused hands and grimy skin of a hardened miner, and he felt it was time to move on.

In the Assay Office in Helena Rob queued up with a crowd of other miners to change his gold-dust for cash. To his astonishment, the little bag of gold-dust fetched fifty dollars. In one week he'd earned the equivalent of nearly two months' pay for a Mountie—if you got it, thought Rob, remembering the long delayed payroll. He hoped it had finally reached Fort Macleod in safety.

Rob sold his pony, took a room in a cheap boarding house, and did his best to act like a miner on the spree. In the days that followed, he spent long hours making the round of the Helena saloons. Since he spent freely, he soon made plenty of new friends. No one seemed to notice that he bought far more drink for others than he actually swallowed himself.

Whenever he got the chance, Rob worked the conversation round to the Cypress Hills massacre. But two years was a long time in a frontier town, and the population was changing constantly. No one seemed to know or care much about a few Indians getting shot a couple of years ago. Such incidents were too common to cause any lasting interest.

Finally Rob struck lucky. One night a drunken cowboy claimed to have actually met someone who had taken part in the Cypress Hills massacre.

'Skinny little feller called Seth Hayter. Works in a saloon in Fort Benton. Way he tells it, them Indians was just mowed down, women and kids too.' The cowboy shook his head in disgust. 'Hell, even an Indian deserves better than that.'

The cowboy could tell him no more, and soon rode away with his friends. Rob decided it was time to leave Helena and see what he could learn in Fort Benton. At least he had one name to work on—Seth Hayter.

He had enough money to buy a ticket on the stage, but it struck him that it might be safer to make a more inconspicuous arrival, befitting his role as a drifter, wandering aimlessly from place to place. He asked around the saloons and learned that a mule-train was leaving Helena for Benton in a couple of days' to pick up a shipment of goods from the East.

Rob found the head mule-skinner and asked for a job as relief driver, offering to work free in return for the ride to Fort Benton. The west was full of young men roaming from place to place, and the driver accepted his offer willingly enough. He was a thin melancholy individual with buck teeth that made him look very like one of his own mules. 'You ever driven mules before, boy?'

Rob shook his head. 'I've driven oxen though. There's nothing worse than that.'

The driver chuckled. 'You'll learn. Ain't *nothing* more ornery than my mules.' He seemed almost proud of it.

As the mule train rattled its way to Fort Benton, Rob came to agree with him. The mules were devilish beasts, and made several determined attempts to bite him with their big yellow teeth, or break his leg with a savage kick from their powerful hooves. But Rob was determined to stand no nonsense. He soon learned to crack the mule-skinner's whip, producing the pistol-like report that kept the long-eared beasts rattling along.

Since the wagons were empty, it was a quick trip into Fort Benton. Rob saw the mules into their stables and said goodbye to them with relief. Dodging a farewell bite from the lead-mule, he wandered out into the crowded streets. He had visited the busy frontier town before, but that had been well over six months ago, and he was confident no one would remember him. Doggedly he started on yet another round of saloons, talking to barman after barman, asking about a man called Seth Hayter, saying simply that he had a message for him.

It wasn't till the morning of the third day that he had any luck. A white-aproned barman, polishing his bar counter, said, 'Hayter? Believe our swamper's called Hayter. He don't come in till evening though . . .'

A swamper was a general odd job man. Every saloon had one to sweep the floor, clear the tables, empty the spittoons, and do any job the barmen considered beneath them.

Rob took care to be in the saloon that evening, just before the evening rush. Nursing his glass of beer at a corner table, Rob saw a thin, seedy-looking, middle-aged man report for duty, and collect his apron and broom from behind the bar. Before starting work the man looked appealingly at the barman, who grinned and poured him a beer. The man grabbed the glass and emptied it. Then he shuffled off to begin his duties.

Rob watched the man closely. Hayter was a slow and messy worker, spending as much time lounging about and chatting as he dared. As the saloon filled up with cowboys, miners, soldiers, trappers, Hayter hung round on the fringes of each little group smiling greasily, and from time to time someone would buy him a drink. Rob noticed Hayter made a practice of whipping away any glass with a few dregs in it and drinking the contents on his way back to the bar. Half-way through the evening the man was already staggering drunk.

Rob fetched a bottle of whisky and two glasses from the bar and returned to his own table. He poured two glasses, leaving his own untouched before him, and waited till Hayter passed by. Rob waved a hand at the other glass, 'Care to join me in a drink?'

Hayter looked at him blearily, unable to believe his ears.

'Friend of mine hasn't turned up,' said Rob. 'No sense in wasting good whisky. Help yourself.'

Hayter sat down unsteadily, picked up the glass, drained it and after a quick glance at Rob, poured himself another. Rob began, 'You're Seth Hayter, aren't you?' The man nodded, as if surprised anyone should know his name. 'Aren't you the one who was in that battle with the Indians, up in the Cypress Hills?'

The man stared suspiciously. Hurriedly Rob went on. 'Got your name from a cowpuncher in Helena. I'd certainly like to hear about that battle. Must have been quite a fight.'

'I don't like to talk about it.' Hayter drained his second drink.

Rob said, 'Well, it was a while ago. Suppose you've forgotten all about it?'

Hayter spoke bitterly. 'Forgotten? No, I've not forgotten. I only wish I could.' Hayter filled his glass again, but this time he didn't empty it straight away. He sat cradling it in his hands, gazing into its depths like a crystal ball. 'No, I haven't forgotten. The shots and the yelling and the screaming ... I still dream about it.' He looked up at Rob fiercely. 'I used to be a buffalo hunter, you know that? Buffalo hunter, wolfer, trapper. One of the best. I lost my nerve, after ... Couldn't hardly bear to fire a gun, couldn't hit anything if I did.'

Rob nodded. Despite the horror of what this man had done, he was such a wreck that it was impossible not to feel some sympathy for him. Rob didn't much relish trying to pry information out of this pitiful creature, but he had a job to do. 'What about the others who were with you? I suppose it got them in the same way?'

Hayter shook his head. 'Hell, no,' he said bitterly. Shelton is an outlaw anyway. He enjoys killing. Jim Mason ain't bothered any. Or you take Frank Chalmers. He's a big man these days. Ain't no dead Indians keeping him from his sleep...'

A shadow fell over the table and a throaty voice said, 'Gentleman of leisure now, are we, Seth? Taking our ease with the customers?' Rob looked up. A very big, very fat man was looming over their table. From his expensive black suit, and the equally expensive rings on his fingers, Rob guessed him to be the owner. Hayter leaped to his feet, 'Sorry, Mr Mason. Young feller here offered me a drink. Be rude to refuse.' Hayter scuffled away, and busied himself clearing glasses from nearby tables.

Mason said, 'You're taking a lot of interest in my help, mister.'

Rob tried to look surprised. 'I just bought the man a drink. He started telling me some tale about killing Indians.'

Mason nodded. 'Seth talks too much.'

'That's what I thought. I reckoned he was just making it up.'

'You go right on thinking that, mister. It's a lot healthier.' The big man turned away and went back to the bar. Rob waited a minute or two, then slipped out by a side entrance.

At the bar one of Mason's barmen was saying, 'Sure, I remember. He was in earlier asking about Seth. Said he had a message for him.'

'And now he comes in asking him questions. Buys a bottle of whisky and don't touch it himself...' Mason turned to one of his hangers-on. 'Put the word out. When Skelton gets back to town, I want to see him, urgent. Tell him someone's been asking questions. And start looking for that kid. I want to know who he is!'

Rob went to sleep that night in an optimistic mood. He'd found two of the men he was looking for and learned the names of two more. Tomorrow he'd start searching for them.

What Rob had failed to realise was the amount of suspicion he'd aroused. By now the men he hunted were hunting for him.

8

'We're going to kill you'

Next morning as he wandered the streets of Fort Benton, Rob felt considerably less optimistic. The main trouble was he had no official position. He carried a letter of authority from Macleod, but didn't dare to use it. The warning of the Sheriff of Helena made it clear that he could expect no help from the law. He had two men to look for. Skelton the outlaw, and Frank Chalmers, who had been described by Hayter as 'a big man these days'. Presumably that meant someone of substance, a rancher, a banker, possibly a merchant.

Because it was the easiest, Rob decided to start with the last group. He wandered up and down the main streets, looking at store-fronts.

'Just you look where you're going, young man.' Rob had bumped into an old lady in a poke bonnet, spilling all her parcels.

'Sorry, ma'am,' he said humbly, and bent to help her pick them up.

'What do you think you're doing,' she scolded him, 'wandering along with your head in the clouds. Careless, that's the trouble with young folks today...'

Rob looked at her thoughtfully. She was a bright-eyed, bird-like old lady, reminding him of his Great-Aunt Wilhemina back home. Great-Aunt Wilhemina knew everything about everybody for miles around.

Maybe this old lady was the same.

'Sorry I bumped into you, ma'am. Thing is, I work on a ranch just outside town. And my boss sent me in with a message for Mr Frank Chalmers.' Rob scratched his head and grinned foolishly. 'Only with the noise and the people and all, I clean forgot Mr Chalmers' address.'

The old lady looked delighted, as if this confession had confirmed all her fears of the younger generation. 'Typical,' she squawked. 'Typical. Forget your head next.' She pointed across the muddy street. 'That's Mr Chalmers' store there. The big new building on the corner.'

Rob said meekly, 'Thank you, ma'am,' and touched his battered hat. He crossed the street and looked up at the building. The sign outside, freshly painted in ornate gold lettering, read, 'New Helena Emporium. F. Chalmers, Proprietor.' On sudden impulse, Rob went inside.

He found himself in a big square room, counters running along three sides. Racks and shelves all round the room were stacked high with all the hundred and one necessities of frontier life. There were tools, barrels of nails, rolls of wire, crates of crockery, agricultural implements, guns, knives, fishing gear, work clothes and fancy clothes for Sunday best. Judging by the way the throng of customers were keeping the counter clerks busy, Mr Chalmers was doing good business.

One of the clerks, a fussy middle-aged man, noticed Rob loitering about, and said sharply, 'Yes, young man?' It was obvious that Rob with his worn clothing and work-grimed hands, wasn't the sort of customer the Emporium welcomed.

Irritated by the man's manner, Rob said, 'I'm looking for Mr Chalmers.'

'Indeed? May one ask why?'

'I've a message for him. It's very urgent.'

'And what's this urgent message about?'

'Why don't you ask Mr Chalmers? He'll tell you if he wants you to know.'

The clerk looked at Rob dubiously. 'All right. Wait here.' He went through a door behind the counter. After a minute he reappeared, followed by a stocky man with thinning sandy hair.

The newcomer beckoned Rob over and said, 'Yes?' in a brisk, no-nonsense voice.

Rob said, 'The message is private.'

The man hesitated a moment, then nodded to Rob to follow him. The little door behind the counter led into a tiny, cluttered office. Once they were inside he said, 'Well?'

Rob looked at him carefully. For all his prosperous air and bossy manner, there was something rather furtive and shifty about Mr Chalmers. It was almost as though he himself didn't quite believe in the front he was putting up. He looked like a man who could be bluffed. Rob deliberately let his coat fall open to reveal the Colt stuck in his waistband. He made his voice tough and insolent. 'No need to get uppity, Chalmers. I was paid to bring you a message.'

'What message? What's it about?'

'About some Indians got themselves killed, in the Cypress Hills a couple of years back.'

96

Rob saw at once that he'd scored a hit. Agitatedly Chalmers said, 'Who are you? Who sent you here?'

'Who I am don't concern you. As for who sent me, he just said it was an old friend.'

'What was his name?'

'He didn't give one. Maybe he reckoned you'd guess.' Chalmers wiped sweat from his brow with a fancy silk handkerchief.

'What did he look like?'

Rob decided it was time to gamble. From Jerry Potts' account, the leader of the men who'd ambushed them for the payroll had been the long-haired one who escaped. And Rob was sure that the threats of the fat outlaw about 'minding their own affairs' had referred to their prying into the Cypress Hills massacre. Which could mean the long-haired man was involved ... Rob took a deep breath and said, 'Tall thin feller, kinda skull-like face. Long yellow hair.'

Another hit. Chalmers gasped, 'Skelton! What did he say?'

Rob paused, working out his story. 'He said to tell you some fellers came over the border from Canada, went to see the Sheriff in Helena. They're talking about extraditing everyone involved in the Cypress Hills business, so they can stand trial in Canada.'

Chalmers stood up and began pacing about. 'They can't, not after all this time.' He grabbed Rob's arm as if trying to convince him. 'You've seen this store. Finest place in Helena, built it up myself from nothing. I can't lose it all now. I'll have to move out...'

Rob thought rapidly. Having found one of his

men, the last thing he wanted to do was scare him off.

'Your friend said that's just what you mustn't do. Sit tight and wait till you hear from him. He's fixing things so there won't be any trouble.' Rob paused. Now he was coming to the most important part of his bluff. Casually he added, 'He wanted me to warn the others as well. I've already spoken to Mason and Hayter, now I've seen you. Can you tell me where the rest hang out?'

Chalmers looked puzzled. 'That only leaves the Sedgewick boys. They're still on their ranch west of town. There was only seven of us and Ed Bishop was killed. Didn't Skelton tell you?'

'Oh sure,' said Rob airily. 'Just wanted to check. Well, I'll be moving on.' Before Chalmers could stop him, or ask more questions, Rob strode out of the office, through the store, and disappeared into the street. Chalmers ran to the shop door and called after him, but Rob had already melted into the crowd.

Slowly Frank Chalmers walked back into his shop. Ignoring the curious looks from his clerks he went into his tiny office and sank into a chair. Weak as he was, Chalmers was far from stupid. Something about his visitor just hadn't rung true. Why should Skelton have paid someone to bring him a warning and then tell him to do nothing? It wasn't much like Skelton to bother about anyone else's skin. But if his visitor hadn't come from Skelton, what had he been up to?

Chalmers sat brooding for almost an hour, ignoring the business of the store, sending away any of the clerks who tried to talk to him. Suddenly the door to his office was flung open. He looked up angrily, 'I thought I said no one was to——' His voice died away. A tall thin man with long yellow hair stood lounging against the doorway. His skin was stretched tight over the bones of his face giving him a curiously skull-like look. He kicked the door closed behind him.

Chalmers rose slowly to his feet. 'Skelton! I don't get it—your man was just here...'

The tall man's smile made him look more like a death's head than ever. 'What man was that?' Terrified, Chalmers poured out the whole story.

Rob made straight for a livery stable and bought a mangy grey cow pony. It was an ugly-tempered brute, but looked as if it had plenty of endurance. He bought a cheap, second-hand saddle, panniers and the rest of the gear he needed, stocked up with supplies, and in just over an hour was riding down the trail from Fort Benton, heading for the Canadian border.

Rob was feeling jubilant. He'd succeeded in his mission better than he'd ever dared hope. Starting from nothing he had six names. Skelton, the long-haired outlaw who'd tried to steal the payroll. Mason the saloon-keeper, and the wretched, drunken swamper, Hayter. Chalmers in his store and the Sedgewick brothers on their ranch outside town. Rob considered visiting the Sedgewick ranch, but decided it was too dangerous. He didn't want to ruin everything at the last minute. The sooner he got back to Macleod with those six names the better. Always provided Jerry Potts had found the missing Abe Farwell, the Commissioner could have the men extradited straight away.

Rob pushed on as far as he could that first day, wanting to put as much distance as possible between himself and Fort Benton. But daylight went at last, and he made camp in a clump of trees just off the trail. He was heating some beans over his tiny camp-fire when he heard riders coming towards him. Quickly Rob stamped out the fire, and moved closer to his horse, stroking its nose to quieten it. He could ride on, but decided it would be safer to wait until the riders had passed by. From his hiding place Rob crouched watching the trail intently as the riders came nearer. There were five of them bunched closely together. They rode past and disappeared into the darkness. Rob gave a sigh of relief. He wondered what they were doing on the trail so late. Still at least they didn't seem interested in him.

He was about to relight his camp-fire when he sensed rather than heard a movement behind him. He spun round and caught a glimpse of long yellow hair and a bony, skull-like face. There was a brief flash of metal as a gun barrel crashed down on his head.

A long time later Rob woke up, not because he wanted to, but because someone was digging him brutally in the ribs with a heavy boot. He opened his eyes with an immense effort. He was lying on the mud floor of a small bare room. There was a wooden table, a few benches and a big iron stove. He tried to sit up but found he couldn't move. His arms and legs were tied. He shook his head to clear it and looked up. Six faces stared down at him. Four of them he recognised at once. Hayter and Mason from the saloon. Chalmers the storekeeper. And Skelton, the long-haired outlaw who had struck him down. The last two men were bow-legged and broad-shouldered. Their heavy, brutal faces bore a strong family resemblance. The rasping voice of Skelton confirmed his thoughts. 'In case you're wondering where you are, you're on the Sedgewick boys' place—that's Tim and Mike there. If you're trying to think up a good story, don't bother—we found this.' Skelton held up Macleod's letter of authority. 'And if you're wondering what we're going to do with you—we're going to kill you.'

Mason, the saloon keeper, was the next to speak. 'The thing is, Mountie, we've got no choice. We've got to protect ourselves.' He seemed genuinely anxious to convince Rob they were only being reasonable. 'We were all in the Cypress Hills thing together. Maybe we acted a mite hasty. We'd been drinking some, and Skelton here egged us on. He never did like Indians. Still that's all in the past. When it was over, we kinda split up. Didn't seem to get along so well with each other any more. I went into the saloon business, Seth Hayter came to work for me, Chalmers started his store, Tim and Mike here came back to their spread and stocked it up—with a little help from their neighbours!' The two brothers grinned. Mason nodded towards the long-haired man. 'Skelton went back on the dodge, same as always.' The fat man sighed. 'Well, we all went our different ways and some of us did pretty well. Then you came along. Seeing as one of us is a drunk and another a blabbermouth,' he looked from Hayter to Chalmers, 'pretty soon you got on to us. Well, too bad for you, 'cause we ain't giving everything up for a few dead Indians. So, like I say, we got to kill you.'

Rob struggled against his bonds. He felt too angry to be afraid, angry at his own stupidity in getting captured, angrier still at the thought that these men might get away with their crimes. He managed to speak, though his throat was dry. 'It won't do you any good,' he croaked. 'They'll send someone else.'

'Maybe they will. But this time we'll be ready for him. He won't even get near us.'

Mason was obviously fond of the sound of his own voice, and Skelton grew impatient. 'We're wasting time. Might as well get it over with.' He drew his revolver.

'No!' Mason's voice was firm. 'We don't want any bullet wounds on the body.'

Skelton lowered his gun. 'Then what do we do with him?'

'Take him to the river and throw him in. They'll probably never find the body, but if they do it'll look like an accident!'

Skelton nodded approvingly. 'Who's going to do it?' There was an uneasy silence. Skelton laughed contemptuously. 'Sure, leave the dirty work to me. You boys are too lily-white to dirty your hands these days.'

One of the Sedgewick brothers spoke, 'Say, you can borrow our rig, make it easier for you.'

Mason cleared his throat. 'Well, we'd better be getting back.' All six men filed out of the room. No one looked at Rob; they ignored him as if he was already dead. Soon the brothers returned, picked Rob up and carried him out into the yard. They threw him in the back of a buckboard, Skelton took the reins and drove away from the little ranch-house.

The journey was a long one, and Rob used every minute of it to plan his escape. He struggled desperately with his bonds but couldn't shift them. That left only one chance of escape. If Skelton wanted his death to look like an accident, he'd have to take the ropes off before he threw him in.

The buckboard jolted to a halt and Rob heard the sound of rushing water. Skelton rolled him out over the end of the buckboard and he thudded to the ground. Rob forced himself to go completely limp. 'End of the line,' said Skelton's voice, and a toe thudded into his ribs. Rob didn't move or stir. Seemingly satisfied that Rob had passed out again, Skelton began undoing the knots. Rob forced himself to stay completely motionless. Even when arms and legs were free he didn't stir. Only when the outlaw was dragging him towards the sound of rushing water did he suddenly come to life, twisting from his grasp and starting to make a run for it. But his legs, cramped from being tied so long, refused to carry him. He managed only a few stumbling steps before Skelton grabbed hold of him again. Rob struggled desperately but the man was too strong. He manhandled him to what seemed a kind of cliff edge and for a moment they both struggled wildly on the brink. Skelton drew his gun and slashed down. Rob felt a searing pain on the side of his head, a sudden sensation of flying through space, then icy rushing waters closed over his head and he was swept away downstream.

9

Escape

As soon as he struck water Rob felt the powerful tug
of the current. He struck out desperately for the
shore, but managed only a few strokes before being
swept away. He was tumbled over and over, gasping
for air. At last his head bobbed clear. He drew in a
deep gasping breath and started swimming again.
This time he managed to struggle closer to the bank.
He felt the muddy bottom for a moment and then the
current knocked him off his feet again.

There was a fallen tree by the river bank, blown
down in some storm, its bare branches trailing in the
water. The rushing current carried Rob down stream
and he stuck in its branches. He hung there gasping
for a moment then started working his way along the
trunk towards the shore. Suddenly he heard footsteps
moving along the river bank.

Shivering, Rob crouched lower in his hiding
place. He guessed Skelton was checking up to make
quite sure Rob was still in the river. In that final
struggle, Rob had managed to dodge the worst effects
of the blow from the outlaw's pistol. It had torn his
ear and bruised his scalp, but he had still been fully
conscious when he entered the water. Otherwise he
would have been dead by now, his body swept far
away down stream. The footsteps came closer, and
Rob saw Skelton approaching, revolver in hand. The

outlaw looked enormous against the night sky, and the long yellow hair turned the skull-like face into a kind of death-mask.

As the man peered about him, Rob grabbed hold of a tree-branch and forced himself to duck deep under water. He crouched there as long as he could until bursting lungs forced him to surface. Then he bobbed his head out of the water and took a few cautious breaths. He could still hear the sound of footsteps, but this time they were moving away. Skelton had passed by without seeing him.

Rob crouched by the fallen tree as long as he could, but soon the icy cold creeping through his body told him he would freeze to death if he didn't move on. Clawing his way up the fallen tree, Rob staggered on to the trail that ran beside the river. Immediately he set off in a stumbling run, striking away from the trail and across the prairie. By now he was pretty well delirious. A part of his mind was aware that his situation was still very bad. After a soaking in the river, he wasn't likely to survive a night in the open. Unless he found help soon, he might as well have stayed in the river. Some primitive instinct for survival made him keep going, stumbling on blindly as long as he could force himself to move.

When he saw the bright spot of the camp-fire ahead of him his mind almost refused to accept it. He staggered closer, and a sharp challenge rang out. 'Just hold it right there, mister.'

Rob was too dazed to take the instruction in, and kept coming forward. He heard the click of a revolver-hammer being thumbed back. 'I said hold it!' Rob took two lurching steps forward and collapsed beside the fire.

This time his awakening was far more pleasant. He found himself on a hard bunk bed, a blanket thrown over him. He heard a voice, 'He's coming to. We'd better get the boss.'

Wrapping a blanket round him, Rob managed to sit up. He was alone in the bunkhouse of a ranch, rows of empty beds all around him. Daylight was streaming through the door and he guessed the cowhands were already out working. His own clothes, washed and dried, were piled at the bottom of the bed, and Rob started getting into them. He had just finished dressing when a tough-looking, grey-haired man marched into the bunkhouse. He looked grimly down at Rob. 'Well, feller, start talking. I want to know why you were wandering around on my range like a drowned rat.'

Rob said, 'Could you tell me where I am—and who you are?'

'Dan Benedict. You're on my spread. Boys found you wandering last night and brought you in. Said you'd been in the river.'

Rob glanced at the old rancher's weather-beaten face. He looked a tough character all right, but he also looked thoroughly honest. Rob decided to trust him. 'Well, Mr Benedict, it's like this...' Rob gave the rancher a simplified version of his adventures—saying he was a member of the North-West Mounted Police working undercover on the trail of some wanted men. The trail had taken him to the ranch of the Sedgewick brothers, who had proved to be friends of the men he was after, and had helped one of them to try and kill him.

As soon as Rob mentioned the Sedgewicks he knew Benedict was on his side. 'I'd believe anything you like to tell me about those two,' he growled. 'Just the two of them on that pint-sized ranch of theirs. They spend most of their time boozing in town. But every round-up, there's a nice fat herd to go to the railhead. Mavericks from *my* herd with *their* brand slapped on ...' This was an old cause of trouble between ranchers. The smaller outfits often reckoned un-branded calves on the range were fair game for the first man to find and brand them, while the bigger, more organised spreads saw things rather differently. 'That's why I had my boys out on the range,' Benedict went on. 'If ever I catch those Sedgewicks running off my cows ... If you're out to get them, I'll give you any help I can. We'll go into Helena and see the sheriff right away.'

Rob shook his head. 'I'd sooner not, sir. At the moment the Sedgewicks and their friends think I'm dead, and I'd like it to stay that way. I've got the names I need and I don't want them frightened off.'

'Then what *do* you want?'

'To get back to Fort Macleod as soon as ever I can. Commissioner Macleod will take it from there.'

The old rancher grumbled and growled. He was all for taking a posse out to the Sedgewick place and dealing with them himself. Finally Rob persuaded him to wait. Once convinced, the rancher acted with true Western hospitality, providing Rob with a fresh horse, all the supplies he needed, and a guide to set him on his way.

Soon, an enormous breakfast inside him, Rob was once more heading for the border.

Commissioner Macleod looked down from his great height at the tubby little man trembling before him. 'I understand your reluctance, Mr Farwell, indeed I do. But I personally guarantee your safety. You see,' Macleod's voice was persuasive, 'you, sir, are our only hope of bringing these men to justice. You *saw* what happened there in the Cypress Hills. We intend to establish a rule of law here in Canada, to make sure that this sort of atrocity can never occur again. Securing the arrest of these men will be a big step towards that goal, but I can't do it without your help.'

As Macleod came to the end of his speech, he glanced across at Jerry Potts, who was lounging in his usual place by the door. Jerry never came very far into a room, as though he needed to feel he could always get out quickly if necessary. He had gone on a long and dangerous journey to track down Abe Farwell and bring him back to Fort Macleod. Probably no other white man could have done it. Jerry had gone from one Indian village to another, moving unafraid and unharmed amongst thousands of savage warriors. It had been hard to find Farwell, harder still to persuade him to come back to the Fort. Now Jerry had done his part. The rest was up to Macleod.

Fortunately the strength of the Commissioner's

personality finally did its work, and Farwell agreed, although still reluctantly, to testify against the murderers—if Macleod could find them. There, of course, lay the difficulty. 'You're sure you don't know anything more about them, Mr Farwell?' Macleod persisted.

Farwell shook his head. 'I never saw them before—before that night. They didn't use names much. All I can tell you is they came from Fort Benton.'

'But you *would* recognise them again?'

Farwell shuddered, remembering the screaming and the shooting, the sweating intent faces of the men. 'Oh yes, I'd recognise them. I'll remember every last one of their faces till the day I die.'

Macleod sent for a constable and gave orders for Farwell to be installed in the guest quarters and well looked after. When the little man was gone, he turned to Jerry. 'It's like having half the pieces in a jigsaw puzzle ... useless without the other half. Farwell knows the faces, but unless Rob can come up with the names there's nothing we can do.'

Jerry said confidently, 'Don't worry. Rob come back.'

'It's been a long time now,' said Macleod gloomily. 'If the men he's after find out who he is they'll have no hesitation in killing him. Maybe I should never have sent him.'

Jerry repeated obstinately, 'You see. Rob come back with names.'

The next morning Macleod was crossing the compound when he heard Jerry call from the look-out platform, 'Rider coming! Don't I tell you Rob come back?'

The Commissioner was a different man at the conference in his office that morning. He rubbed his hands together and boomed, 'I knew you'd do it. Didn't I say so, Jerry?' The scout grinned.

Macleod turned back to Rob. 'We'll set out for Fort Shaw immediately. You, me, Jerry and Mr Farwell. We'll collect a military escort in Fort Benton and lock the scoundrels up while I apply for extradition.'

Rob spent just one night in his old barrack room before getting back into uniform and setting out on the trail again. He found his old friends in a far more cheerful mood than when he'd left. The return of Macleod with the payroll had put money in their pockets, and the arrival of a wagon load of goods from an enterprising trader in Fort Benton had given them something to spend it on. Further supplies of food and equipment had arrived too, and the Fort was a different place. Even the melancholy Evans, something of a hero after his sufferings on the payroll journey, reckoned that life in the Mounties wasn't so bad after all.

'You should stay with us for a while, see what it's like,' teased Fred Denbow as they watched Rob preparing to set off yet again.

'Precisely,' said Henri. 'These flying visits of yours, they do not give you the true flavour of Mounted Police life!'

Rob grinned, accepting their teasing good-humouredly. He wanted nothing better than to settle down to the normal life of a Mounted Policeman, and the sooner the better. Once this business was over, maybe he could get on with his proper work.

They had a good journey back to Fort Benton. As he rode along, now in uniform again, Rob felt a different man from the hunted fugitive of recent weeks. Spring was well on the way, and sunshine and warmer weather seemed to reflect his good spirits.

At Macleod's request, Jerry timed their arrival in Fort Benton for just after dark. The Fort was outside town, and the Commanding Officer, a grey-haired, cavalry colonel, was by no means delighted with his unexpected visitors. He stared dubiously at Macleod. 'Surely this is a matter for the civil power,' he grumbled. 'The sheriff in Fort Benton is the man you want.'

Macleod smiled. 'My information is that the civil power is not exactly reliable in matters of this kind,' he said blandly. 'All I ask is your assistance in making sure the sheriff does his duty. I realise my men and I have no status this side of the border. But since this is an official request for assistance from a friendly power, on a matter of importance to both our countries, I'm sure your Government would want you to co-operate.'

The Colonel seemed crushed by the weight of this impressive speech, and as usual Macleod got his way. It was arranged that they should make the arrests first thing in the morning.

Rob, Jerry and Abe Farwell spent the night as guests of the U.S. Cavalry. Spare beds were found for them in one of the barrack rooms. They found their hosts a tough, hard-bitten lot. Privately Rob thought their discipline and turn-out on the casual side by Mountie standards. On the other hand, these men had been fighting for most of their military lives, in the Civil War and the Indian Wars that followed, so perhaps they had some justification for cutting down on spit and polish. Anyway, the troopers were hospitable enough. The guests were given a supper of beefsteak, potatoes and sweet pancakes covered in maple syrup, that made Rob think ruefully of the tea, bread and flapjacks of Fort Macleod. When the meal was over, Rob and Abe Farwell turned in straight away. Jerry got into a poker game, and spent most of the night relieving his hosts of their hard-earned pay.

Commissioner Macleod, meanwhile, was the official guest of the officers' mess. Some of the younger officers, egged on by a certain Lieutenant Kiley, had decided to impress their guest from over the border with the superior toughness of the U.S. Cavalry. They planned to do this by the simple process of drinking him under the table. They could scarcely have picked a worse subject than the burly Commissioner. Macleod had a head like a rock, and his capacity for hard liquor had been the wonder of brother officers throughout his military career. One by one the challengers slipped away, some walking carefully from the room, others sliding gracefully under the table. When the festivities were over it was Macleod who considerately helped Lieutenant Kiley from the room, and steered him towards his bed.

By a sort of poetic justice, it was Lieutenant Kiley who was paraded with his troop next morning to provide Macleod with an escort. The young officer was more than a little pale, and he saw Macleod's lips twitch beneath his moustache at the sight of him.

Kiley took his place beside Macleod at the head of the column, with Rob and Jerry just behind.

The double line of blue-clad cavalrymen formed up, and the little cavalcade rode out of the barracks and towards the town.

It had taken a long time for the law to catch up with the Cypress Hills murderers, thought Rob, but it looked as if their time had come at last.

10

'Throw down that rifle'

The events of that morning were talked about for a long time in Fort Benton. It was normal enough to see a cavalry patrol jingling through the streets. But who were those men in scarlet coats? And why were they stopping at the sheriff's office?

They found Sheriff Hancock eating his breakfast. Macleod explained the situation briefly and forcibly. 'We are going to arrest these men immediately. Lieutenant Kiley and his soldiers will give you any needed assistance. My men and I are merely present as observers. Shall we go, sheriff?' The sheriff looked at Macleod and Kiley. Their faces were grim and determined. He could see the double line of cavalrymen in the street outside. Whatever his private feelings, he knew he was outmanoeuvred. The sheriff sighed, and reached for his gun-belt.

'Looks like you got things all figured out, gents. Let's get moving.'

They picked up Chalmers first. He was in his office, counting the previous day's takings, and at the sight of Rob in Mountie uniform, he jumped up in panic, knocking the cash-box off his desk so that coins spilled unregarded over the floor. The sheriff read out the charges and Chalmers listened in a daze, never taking his eyes from Rob. Two of the troopers were detailed to take him back to the Army Post.

Mason too was checking his takings when the sheriff walked through the door. He looked up in surprise. 'Morning, sheriff. Kinda early for you, isn't it?' The smile faded from Mason's face when he saw Rob and Macleod, behind the sheriff, and his hand began to move under his coat.

The sheriff said, 'Don't go for that gun, Mason. I'd hate to have to shoot an old friend. Anyway, there's soldiers all round your place.'

Mason slowly put his hands on the counter. Which was just as well for him, thought Rob, since Jerry's revolver was already drawn and cocked.

Hayter came shuffling into the saloon, broom in hand. 'I finished up out back, Mr Mason...' His voice tailed away as he saw the roomful of men. He stayed silent and shaking while the sheriff read the charges out and went meekly with the soldiers who took him away, unlike Mason who kept up a steady stream of curses and threats.

As they rode out of town, Rob reflected that the last part of the operation looked like being the most difficult. The Sedgewick brothers and the outlaw Skelton were by far the toughest of the wanted men, and the most likely to offer armed resistance.

Lieutenant Kiley split his small force into four, sending men to cover the back and both sides of the ranch buildings before leading the remainder, plus Macleod and his party, up to the front of the ranch house.

The little ranch lay silent and peaceful in the morning sunshine. Rob found it hard to believe that a few nights ago he had been gagged, bound and helpless on its floor while his enemies plotted to kill him. Things were very different now. At a nod from Kiley, one of the troopers dismounted and kicked open the front door. Mike Sedgewick was revealed, frying bacon in a pan over the stove. At the sight of soldiers he hurled the pan at the nearest head and dived for his gun-belt which hung over a chair. The angry troopers jumped him, and he disappeared beneath a pile of determined men. A few minutes' later they dragged him kicking and cursing on to the porch. 'All right, Mike,' said the sheriff. 'Where's your brother?'

His only reply was a barrage of curses. Lieutenant Kiley grinned and turned to his sergeant. 'Sergeant, take some men and search the buildings.'

Before the sergeant could obey, the door to the nearby bunkhouse creaked open and Tim Sedgewick staggered out, rubbing his eyes still bleary with sleep. He blinked dazedly at them for a moment, then dashed back inside the bunkhouse, reappearing almost at once with a rifle in his hands. 'You turn my brother loose and clear out,' he yelled.

By now the sheriff had drawn his gun, as had Rob and several of the troopers. 'Drop that gun, Tim,' ordered the sheriff. 'We got men all round the ranch, you'll never make it.'

'Maybe not, but I'll sure take a few of you with me,' yelled Tim. 'You first, then those Mountie fellers!'

For a moment nobody moved. It was a tricky situation, and Rob thought fast. It was true that there were enough of them to shoot the man down without difficulty. It was also true that he could kill quite a few of them before they got him. Rob became aware that Jerry Potts, beside him just a moment ago, had suddenly faded away. He guessed Jerry was taking steps of his own to deal with the problem and decided to give him some help. He moved a little to one side of the group, covering Sedgewick with his revolver. 'Don't you recognise me?' he called. 'Your friend tried to kill me but he didn't quite make it. Now I've come to get you.'

Sedgewick swung his rifle to cover this new threat. 'Maybe *he* didn't kill you, Mountie, but *I* will. Now get off my land or I start shooting.'

'You'll never make it,' yelled the sheriff. 'Throw down that rifle.'

The gun swung back to the sheriff. With two enemies to cover, Sedgewick was becoming angry and confused. Rob realised that if they pushed him too far he would start shooting blindly.

Suddenly Sedgewick stiffened, dropped the rifle and took a step forward. Jerry Potts stepped out of the doorway behind him, his gun in the man's back. Rob let out a deep breath of relief. As he'd guessed, Jerry had used the distraction of their shouted exchange with Sedgewick to slip through a rear window and come up silently behind his man.

In the moment of relaxation that followed Tim's capture, Rob had a sudden premonition of danger. The most dangerous enemy was still free, possibly hiding near by. He turned to Macleod. 'Don't forget Skelton, sir—the long-haired man. If he's still here——'

The warning came too late. Skelton erupted out of

the barn, mounted on a big black horse, reins between his teeth, blazing guns in both hands. His skull-like face was set in a mad grin and his long yellow hair streamed out behind him. For a moment the sheer shock of the demonic apparition held everyone spellbound. Then they flung themselves to one side as he rode straight at them, bursting through the little group. A rattle of shots pursued him as he disappeared into the distance. 'Get after him,' yelled Kiley, as the sergeant and two of his men ran for their horses, leaped into the saddle and thundered away in pursuit. Kiley turned confidently to Macleod. 'My boys'll get him. He'll run straight into my patrols. They'll stop him.'

But they didn't. They learned later that Skelton had hurled himself on to a waiting patrol, killed one man, shot down the horses of the others and galloped away. His pursuers never caught up with him. Jerry Potts led a tracking party, but for once even he returned empty-handed.

The other prisoners, Chalmers, Hayter, Mason and the two Sedgewicks, were taken back to the barracks. Abe Farwell made a formal deposition identifying them as the men responsible for the massacre. They were handed over to the civil authorities to await trial. Macleod thought this safe enough now that their capture and arrest had become public news.

He thanked the Colonel for his help and refused the offer of another night's hospitality. The Colonel smiled. 'Maybe it's just as well, Commissioner. From what I hear I don't know if my officers could stand another mess dinner like the last.'

Lieutenant Kiley saluted. 'A great pleasure to work with you, sir.'

Macleod gave his urbane smile. 'And my thanks to you both. I found both work *and* relaxation most enjoyable.'

As they took the trail for home Rob asked, 'What happens now, sir? Why didn't we take them back with us?'

'The slow-grinding mills of the law,' answered Macleod. 'First there'll be an extradition hearing, probably in Helena, since that's the state capital. Then they'll have to be taken to Winnipeg for trial by the Canadian Courts.'

Jerry Potts grunted. 'Damn fool nonsense. Why don't we just shoot them?'

'Because those days are over,' said Macleod. 'Law and order means that even their kind must have a fair trial. Don't you agree, Corporal MacGregor?'

'Well, I suppose so, sir,' said Rob. 'Though I see what Jerry...' His voice tailed off as he realised what Macleod had just said. 'Excuse me, sir, you did say...'

'I said *Corporal* MacGregor. You have carried out an important and dangerous mission for the Force. I therefore propose to reward you by giving you a good deal more work, a great deal more responsibility and a very small increase in pay.'

'Yes, sir. Thank you, sir,' said Rob, not daring to say any more.

As they rode homewards Rob's head was full of the excitement of recent events. Now there was promotion to crown it all. In many ways it would make life harder. Inevitably there would be some to make the old charge of favouritism. In addition, it would be bound to put some distance between him and his friends, however much he tried not to let it.

It was a pity about Skelton though. At the barracks in Fort Benton, the other prisoners had united in blaming Skelton for the massacre. Although it was natural enough for them to make a scapegoat of the missing outlaw, Rob felt there was a good deal of truth in the charges. Certainly Skelton had impressed him as the most evil member of the group.

He couldn't help hoping that someday he would see Skelton again. But he had no idea of the strange and gruesome circumstances under which his wish was to be granted.

Epilogue

A Kind of Justice

Corporal MacGregor was away from the Fort in charge of a wood-cutting detail when Commissioner Macleod came back from the extradition hearing in Helena. On Rob's arrival at the Fort, the excited sentry told him of the Commissioner's return. 'Went straight to his quarters, face as black as thunder. No one's seen him since. Left orders for you to report to him soon as you got back.'

Rob saw his wood unloaded from the wagons and safely stowed away, dismissed his work-party, and hurried to the Commissioner's quarters.

Macleod was standing by the stove. He nodded absently in reply to Rob's salute and said, 'At ease, Corporal MacGregor.' He didn't speak for a moment, just stood there scowling blackly. Rob wondered if he'd committed some terrible crime without realising. Were the two gold stripes on his arm to be taken away already? Then Rob realised that Macleod was gazing into the distance. Whatever he was angry about, it had nothing to do with Rob. The Commissioner suddenly focussed his gaze on Rob, as if coming back to reality. He cleared his throat, but still didn't speak. With a sudden shock, Rob realised that Macleod was feeling embarrassed.

Unable to bear the silence any longer, Rob began,

'The extradition hearings in Helena, sir. How did it go?'

Explosively Macleod said, 'Freed! All five of them!'

Rob couldn't take the news in. 'How can they have been, sir—with all the evidence?'

'The trial was a farce. Shouting, yelling, courtroom histrionics. The courtroom was packed with armed men, there were riots and processions in the streets outside ... They turned those men into heroes. Even the District-attorney we hired to prosecute them was openly on their side.'

Rob still couldn't absorb the news. He stared incredulously at the Commissioner, who went on, 'The defendants claimed self-defence. Said they were peaceful trappers attacked by Indians. They were simply protecting their own lives.'

'But what about Abe Farwell's evidence, sir? He saw it all.'

Macleod answered bitterly, 'Mr Farwell, you will recall, has an Indian wife. That apparently makes him unreliable as a witness. Anyway, the United States Commissioner refused extradition.'

Rob nodded slowly, as the bitter news sank in. He remembered what Jerry Potts had said, that in America killing Indians didn't make you a criminal, it made you a hero. The long years of Indian wars had left such a heritage of bitterness that it was hard for many American frontiersmen to accept that Indians were human. Well, thought Rob determinedly, they'd just have to see that the same thing didn't happen here.

Macleod's voice broke in on his thoughts. 'I'm sorry, MacGregor. You did a fine job for us, but it was all for nothing.'

Rob shook his head. 'No, sir. Not for nothing. We said we'd get them, and we did. The whole of Fort Benton saw them taken through the streets under arrest. We did our part.'

'That may be. But will Chief Crowfoot see it like that? I gave him my word that these men would be brought to justice.'

'So they were, sir. It's not your fault if justice let them go again.'

'Obviously Chief Crowfoot will have to be told,' said Macleod heavily. 'He's bound to hear sooner or later, and I'd like him to hear it from us first.'

'I'll go, sir,' volunteered Rob. 'I may as well see it through to the end.'

This time there was no hostile demonstration as Rob and Jerry Potts rode into Crowfoot's camp several days later. Blackfoot hunting parties had brought warnings of their coming, and Rob was taken straight to the Chief's tent. Bluntly Rob told his story, his tracking down of the men, their arrest, and their subsequent release by the court in Helena. Crowfoot listened in silence. When Rob's story was over, the Chief said, 'It was not to be expected that the wolf would turn against his own kind. Tell Macleod I am satisfied. Tell him I will visit him soon, to discuss the treaty.'

Rob felt a tremendous surge of relief. All their

efforts had not been in vain. They had shown the Canadian Indians that when the Police gave their word they kept it. As Rob turned to leave, the Chief said, 'I hope you will stay the night in our camp. My son Red Crow says he has much to tell you.' He smiled. 'I hope he has not been stealing any more horses.'

Red Crow was waiting outside, and he bore Rob off to his own tepee. Rob told his story once more, and the young warrior grunted. 'Justice of white man very strange. Lock Indian up for stealing pony, set white man free for killing Indian.' It was obvious that Red Crow's arrest still rankled and Rob thought it more diplomatic not to reply. Red Crow sat in brooding silence for a while, then said, 'There is something I must show you, my brother. But first take off the red coat.' Puzzled, Rob obeyed, taking off his uniform tunic and wrapping a buffalo robe around his shoulders. Red Crow said, 'I speak now not to the red coat soldier, but to Mas-gwa-ah-sid, brother of the Blackfoot. See!' Red Crow led Rob to the central pole of the tepee and pointed. Rob looked up and gasped. Dangling from the pole by a rawhide thong was a human skull. Somehow the scalp was still attached to the skull, and long greasy yellow hair hung round the bony face. Rob found himself staring at Skelton the outlaw, his features now transformed into the skull they had so much resembled in life. 'He fled from the soldiers across the medicine line, into Blackfoot country,' said Red Crow grimly. 'We were waiting for him. Little Soldier and his people were our brothers.'

Rob looked at the skull of his dead enemy. It was odd the way things had worked out. The men who had been captured were safe and free in Fort Benton. The man who had escaped was here, his sightless eye-sockets gazing from the pole of an Indian tepee.

Rob saw Red Crow looking at him a little anxiously. He realised his Indian friend had wanted him to know that not all the murderers had gone free, and had trusted him with this dangerous secret in order to do so. According to the letter of the law, Rob supposed he should arrest Red Crow and his braves for killing Skelton. But he hadn't the slightest intention of doing so. Let what had happened here balance what had happened in Helena. Perhaps, after all, a kind of justice had been served. Rob went back to his seat on the rug, took off his blanket and put on his tunic. Solemnly he turned to Red Crow, 'They tell me that the buffalo hunt has been good this year.' The subject of Skelton was closed between them.

Rob made his last reference to Skelton and his fate on the following day, when he was getting ready for the ride back to the fort. 'You know, Jerry, I've been thinking. Someone must have warned the Blackfoot to watch out for Skelton. Someone who was a good enough tracker to work out the direction he'd take. Someone the Indians trusted.'

Jerry looked up at him, his black Indian eyes expressionless. Rob went on, 'I remember thinking at the time, it's very unlike you to lose track of a man—unless it suited you.'

Jerry said, 'Sometimes white half don't work so

well. Indian half get things done better. You tell Macleod?'

Rob shook his head. 'He's got enough to worry about already. Come on, we'd better be moving.' They mounted their horses and started back down the long trail to Fort Macleod.

AUTHOR'S NOTE

Like 'The Great March West', the first book in the 'Mounties' series, 'Massacre in the Hills' is fiction based on fact.

There really was a Cypress Hills massacre. The scandal it caused was one of the factors leading to the Canadian Government's decision to form the North-West Mounted Police.

Although I have created my own villains for this story, the result of the real-life extradition hearing in Helena, Montana, was exactly as described in the book.

Commissioner Macleod, Jerry Potts and Chief Crowfoot were real people. Commissioner Macleod and Jerry Potts did make the long and dangerous journey to Helena, Montana, to fetch the Mounties' wages.

You can read more about the adventures of Rob MacGregor in 'Wardrums of the Blackfoot', the next book in the series.